Mr. Michae
51 Wildw
Palmyra, VA

MW00628532

"Come Love with Me"

"Come Love with Me"

AUGUSTINE AS SPIRITUAL GUIDE

Gabriel Quicke

Paulist Press
New York / Mahwah, NJ

Cover image: Fra Angelico, *The Conversion of St. Augustine*. Image from Bridgeman-Giraudon / Art Resource, NY.
Cover and book design by Lynn Else

Library of Congress Cataloging-in-Publication Data
Quicke, Gabriel.
    "Come love with me" : Augustine as spiritual guide / Gabriel Quicke.
        pages cm
    Includes bibliographical references.
    ISBN 978-0-8091-4923-0 (alk. paper) — ISBN 978-1-58768-487-6
    1. Augustine, Saint, Bishop of Hippo. 2. Theology—Early works to 1800. 3. Christian life. 4. Spiritual life—Christianity. 5. Love—Religious aspects—Christianity. I. Title.
    BR65.A9Q54 2015
    230—dc23
                                                                                2014045197

ISBN 978-0-8091-4923-0 (paperback)
ISBN 978-1-58768-487-6 (e-book)

Published by Paulist Press
997 Macarthur Boulevard
Mahwah, New Jersey 07430

www.paulistpress.com

Printed and bound in the
United States of America

To My Parents and My Aunt Alphonsina

Contents

Introduction

SAINT AUGUSTINE AS SPIRITUAL GUIDE

The source for this book is Saint Augustine's *Tractatus in Iohannis Evangelium* (Homilies or *Tractates* on the Gospel according to John), a pastoral work. Augustine's sermons are an important source for the study of his theology and spirituality and are an essential complement to his doctrinal writings.

This book deals with spirituality on a pastoral level. It shows how Augustine presented complex theological thought to the faithful, how he acted as bishop and pastor, and how he tried to promote unity in the Church. This approach reminds us that theology is not only an academic exercise but concerns the life of the people of God. Augustine's preaching and his loving service to the people of his diocese are very significant in his spirituality, which can be understood in terms of his experience of God's love in Christ throughout his pilgrimage of conversion and faith.

Here I attempt to bring the two elements together by going to the heart of Augustine's spirituality and to the heart of the Christian way of life. Through this dual movement, we can discover common links such as prayer, humility, the guidance of the Holy Spirit, the Pilgrim Church, and charity. This book looks both at Augustine in his time and at Christian life today. Although Augustine was a witness for his contemporaries, I hope to show how he can be a witness for Christians today.

Augustine can enlighten us as we seek and yearn for peace and harmony. Looking at the past illuminates the present and is a guide for the future. However, we must avoid oversimplifying the relationship between the past and the present. On the one hand, we must let the past speak for itself. On the other hand, we must distinguish between that which is universally enduring and that which is historically and culturally determined.

This book restricts itself to the study of spiritual themes as outlined in the *Tractatus in Iohannis Evangelium*. The selection of pastoral applications in the concluding chapter is not intended to be exhaustive, but is offered as a range of possible examples. I explain why Augustine, who experienced God's love in the humble Christ and was a witness of Christian unity, can be considered a spiritual guide for today's Christian.

THE SPIRITUALITY OF SAINT AUGUSTINE AS PILGRIMAGE

We can understand Augustine's spirituality in terms of his experience of God's love in Christ during his pilgrimage of conversion and faith. His preaching and loving service to the people of his diocese is very significant for his spirituality. Augustine can be considered a biblical theologian, for we can say that he developed a biblical spirituality rooted in prayerful meditation on the Holy Scriptures. After ordination to the priesthood, he spent six months immersed in studying the Bible. Augustine's spirituality is centered on the worship and love of the Trinity. We ascend to God by imitating the humble Christ, the Divine Physician, who healed humanity of its pride. The Spirit, who is the bond of love between the Father and the Son, is the soul of the Church, through its renewing and unifying activity. Augustine's sermons reveal a profoundly ecclesial character delineating the dynamic spirituality of the Church as Body of Christ in pilgrimage through conversion and purification. For Augustine, charity and its development in the human heart is at the very heart of Christian life and holiness. With the dialogical style of his homilies on the Gospel of Saint John, Augustine develops a "spirituality of togetherness," inviting us to listen together, to pray together, to walk together, to love together, to sing together, in humility, under the inspiring guidance of the Holy Spirit, as a universal community in pilgrimage to the heavenly Jerusalem.

Through his life, conversion, thoughts, pastoral work, and preaching, Augustine gave witness to the inner pilgrimage he undertook, the pilgrimage of the heart. In his writings and sermons, Augustine speaks about Christian life as a long spiritual journey of the restless heart. Augustine's spirituality deals with this dynamism, a holy tension, which inspires our progress, because we are always on the way, as pilgrims, praying and imitating the humble Christ, asking for forgiveness, bearing one another's burdens, walking together, "running by believing and loving."[1]

Today people have rediscovered the practice of pilgrimage. A pilgrimage can be considered as a symbol of our earthly life, which is essentially an extended pilgrimage, constant traveling. In this, pilgrimage has a deep human symbolic significance. In all its trials, temptations, forced detours, and surprising encounters, a pilgrimage is a metaphor, a reflection of human existence as a whole. A human being is a *Homo Viator*—Pilgrim Man.[2] People are driven by the desire to travel, to leave their homes and go on a journey. Every human being is a pilgrim.

Not surprisingly, pilgrimage has existed in all times, in most religions, and in cultures everywhere. The people of Israel journeyed to the temple of Jerusalem. Muslims make pilgrimages to Mecca. Hindus travel to the Ganges River, among other holy places. Buddhists journey from place to place to receive the mercy of Gautama Buddha.

In his *Confessions*, Augustine refers to men who "go forth to wonder at the heights of mountains, the huge waves of the sea, the broad flow of the rivers, the extent of the ocean, and the courses of the stars,"[3] but who neglect to wonder at themselves. Therefore, Augustine encourages a return to the interior of the heart and develops a theology of pilgrimage of the heart. True pilgrimage is not undertaken with feet but with the heart, not with bodily footsteps but with the footsteps of the heart. According to Augustine, the baggage for this journey is humility and love.[4]

Pilgrimage is an important symbol for Christians. As a member of the people of God, the Christian is on the road. Pilgrimage is the symbol of the journey of the people of God throughout the ages. The Christian way of life can be compared to a pilgrim journey. Thus, one can speak of Christians as being on a pilgrimage.

Christianity has a strong tradition of pilgrimage. A famous symbol of pilgrimage is the labyrinth of Chartres in France. The Cathedral of Chartres was built around 1230. The labyrinth in the floor is designed according to a basic pattern: twelve circles that form a single path to a center: the "rosette." The path makes twenty-eight turns, seven from the left to the center, then seven from the right to the center, followed by seven from the left to the outside, followed by seven from the right to the outside. Finally, there is a short path to the rosette. The Middle Ages was a time of pilgrimage, but since it was not possible for many to make a pilgrimage to Jerusalem, they instead went to cathedrals such as Chartres, where they could make the spiritual journey by following the path of the pilgrims' labyrinth.

There can be diverse reasons for making a pilgrimage. There can be personal reasons such as the following: to strengthen one's faith, to pray, to do penance, to ask for the forgiveness of sins, to beg for a favor, to ask for physical or mental healing, to think about the big questions of life, to experience a sense of connectedness or union with nature, the cosmos, fellow pilgrims, with God. Even if there are such personal reasons, the pilgrim joins the preceding generations of pilgrims. In this way, they step into a tradition, undertaking the pilgrimage as a collective act.

Pilgrimage creates a rupture between daily life and the journey. Abraham is the archetype of every Christian pilgrim. He was called by God to leave his homeland, and he went forth from his family to start a new life in the promised land (cf. Gen 12:13). His transformation included a new name, Abraham, as a sign of his new identity.

Each pilgrimage has a rite of transition. The pilgrim exceeds a spatial boundary between two domains. On the one hand, he leaves his house, his family, his city, or country. On the other hand, he enters the realm of the unknown, the other, the new. Therefore, the departure is an act of confidence and trust.

Pilgrimage means changing one's mindset, the result of experiences on the road. The pilgrim is like a stranger who is traveling in a foreign land. He entrusts himself to the hospitality and generosity of people he meets on the road. Along the way, purification takes place; something happens and changes in the depths of the heart. The pilgrim not only undertakes a bodily journey, but also an inner journey, a journey of the heart. En route, the pilgrim is confronted with himself. Pilgrimage becomes the road to repentance, to a revision of one's own life.

On the road, the pilgrim encounters fellow travelers. A bond of solidarity, togetherness, and unity grows, for they are foreigners, yet they are fellow travelers on their way to the same destination. They share the same challenges, the same weather, the experience of hunger and thirst. They also share the same desire to arrive at the destination. They are called to bear each other's burdens, to listen to each other's life story. Together they listen to the story of God through prayer and thanksgiving.

Once we arrive at our destination, we realize that life is not as it was before. We have changed. Throughout purification and repentance, we have drawn closer to each other. The arrival is not the end of the journey, but a new beginning. The pilgrimage continues.

All pilgrimages have common experiences and challenges related to the departure, to the journey itself, and to the longing for the destination. Christian life is a pilgrimage on the way to Jesus' kingdom, a great trek to the heavenly Jerusalem. Christian spirituality can be considered a pilgrimage that we undertake together, not in order to seek a nostalgic return to a mythical past but to identify the way forward, toward the One who calls us to communion, to unity in diversity.

We can say that Augustine tried, in difficult circumstances, to be an advocate for unity of the Church and an apostle of peace in conformity with the evangelical imperative of the love of God and the love of neighbor. The witness that Augustine gave can be a source for Christian life today. Christian spirituality can be considered as a journey toward harmony through prayer, humility, the guidance of the Holy Spirit, the Pilgrim Church, and charity. The dynamic way in which Augustine developed these spiritual themes can be an inspiration for us today. The symbol of the pilgrim's labyrinth of Chartres can help to clarify that Augustine's spirituality can offer us today spiritual food on our pilgrimage toward Christian unity.

CHAPTER I

Minister of the Word

The first spiritual theme in the *Tractates* concerns prayer. Augustine emphasized that preaching begins with and is supported by prayer. The preacher mediates between the Word of God and the faithful. On the one hand, the minister stands face-to-face with God, on the other hand he stands face-to-face with the faithful. Augustine prepared himself at home through meditation and prayer, and did not write out his sermons. In this way, as he preached he could dialogue with the faithful and immediately respond to their comments. Augustine asked the faithful to pray for him that God would give him the right insight and the appropriate words. He prayed simultaneously for the faithful, that they would understand his words well. Augustine's dialogical preaching is based upon listening together to God's Word in silence.

"LET US SEARCH TOGETHER": A DIALOGICAL PREACHING STYLE

Saint Augustine as a Preacher

Despite his poor health, his weak voice, and his insatiable desire for quiet study and meditation, Augustine preached quite often, on average twice a week, usually on Saturday and Sunday, and almost every day during Lent, not only in Hippo, but also in many other places. He might have preached about eight thousand sermons, of which about five hundred are preserved.[1] Augustine's sermons can be divided into three categories: commentaries on the Gospels and the First Letter of John, commentaries on the psalms, and finally the sermons for the liturgical year. The sermons were preached during the eucharistic celebration, after the Bible readings and the singing of the responsorial psalm. Augustine also delivered homilies outside eucharistic celebrations. Unfortunately, we cannot listen to his sermons. We can no longer delight in the timbre of his voice, appreciate his intonation, and perceive his emphasis. What remains is only the text of the sermons written down by stenographers.

Augustine perceived his role as pastor as a serious and difficult task. He undertook his duty as bishop with tireless dedication. "Because of my stress of time I am limiting myself as much as I can for your sakes....The Bishop is speaking a word. I am speaking a word of the Word. But what a word...? A mortal word, of the Word Immortal; a changeable word of the Word Unchangeable; a passing word of the Word Eternal."[2] Preaching was Augustine's main task and was sometimes very fatiguing. On average, the length of a sermon was half an hour, sometimes even longer. Because of his poor health and his weak voice—there were no microphones then—occasionally he had to interrupt his sermon. Sometimes his listeners applauded him. He would often stop the applause, especially when he felt it risked hypocrisy. "I want good behavior from you, no applause."[3]

Augustine called for clarity in preaching. He believed that the Bible should be clearly explained. He often used popular examples intended to touch the human heart with rich visual language. In this respect, the sermons of Augustine are fascinating. Here a real pastor is at work: someone who tries to translate his own faith understanding to the faithful in a simple way. In *On Christian Doctrine*, he made the distinction between the interpretation of a text and the transfer of it to the audience. He did not care only about the meaning of the text, but also how he might explain the content in the best way possible. He wanted to teach, to persuade, and to touch the faithful. Augustine focused explicitly on his audience. He involved the faithful by asking them for attention and patience. He called for a joyful and agreeable atmosphere during teaching and often made a playful remark or a joke.

His remarkable gifts as a preacher and educator, his rhetorical genius, the simplicity of his language, the clarity of his discourses, and the spontaneity of his reactions all inspired a dynamic dialogue with his audience, who responded with their attention. He spoke to their hearts from his heart. He loved the faithful and they loved him. Amid all the labors and dangers of his life, he found joy and consolation in their love for God, their devout zeal, their firm hope, and their fervor of spirit. He usually used friendly and familial names when addressing the faithful. Harsh words were the exceptions in his preaching.

Augustine's audience was diverse and changing.[4] In addition to the baptized, his congregation included cate-chumens. He saw before him the rich and the poor, men and women, widowers and widows, consecrated virgins and ascetics, unmarried young people, and elders. Most, but not all, were illiterate. Augustine complained that he often had to repeat biblical explanations because he was not sure what his hearers would remember. However, Augustine knew that some could read the Scriptures. He invited his audience to read the text in order to check his explanation. He invited his audience to inquire peacefully, without quarreling.

Augustine's attention was mainly attracted by the dif-ferences in the spiritual disposition of his listeners. He referred to people who did not take the Word of God into account, those who were Christian in name only. Sometimes he referred to drunkards, the covetous, idolaters, and thieves. Some Christians engaged in superstitious practices and pagan rituals, and secretly sought out diviners and consulted astrologers. Yet most were people of good will, fervent in spirit, who loved their bishop.

Augustine felt joy and consolation in all the labors and dangers of his life when he observed the love of God, the pious zeal, the assured hope, and fervor of spirit of some of his listeners. Many faithful came to church daily, but Augustine informed them that it was not sufficient to listen to his daily exhortations. There had to be a personal reflection to prepare the field of the heart so that the seed of the Word might take root, germinate, and bring forth the fruit in which the farmer rejoices and delights. Augustine was very happy when he saw how enthusiastically the faithful came together, on fire in the Spirit. He invited them, "Be simple, but only in such wise that you be fervent, and let your fervor be in your tongues. Hold not your peace, speak with glowing tongues, set those that are cold on fire."[5] Augustine encouraged the faithful to build bridges, and he expressed the hope that dialogue could be established among the Christian communities of Hippo.

The religious context of the time was polemical.[6] There was Arianism, named after Arius, an Alexandrian priest who claimed that the Son of God is not equal to the Father, denying the true divinity of Jesus. In 325, the Council of Nicaea condemned this teaching when it affirmed that the Father and the Son are equal and that Jesus is truly God. However, Arianism occupied only a very limited place in his sermons. From 411 on, Augustine became increasingly involved with Pelagianism, a heresy that concerned the relationship between human nature and divine grace. It maintained that the human will is entirely free, and its adherents denied the necessity of redemption and the efficacy of grace. Augustine contrasted their doctrine with orthodox belief and defended the action of divine grace.

Augustine's main concern was Donatism. The Donatists were named after Donatus, bishop of Carthage, and they arose after the great persecution of Christians under Emperor Diocletian. They maintained that sacraments administered by a sinner were invalid, that the value of a sacrament depended on the personal sanctity of the minister. Augustine insisted strongly on the prayer and charity of the faithful to bring the Donatists into the unity of the Church. His approach was very tactful, seeking first to establish dialogue. Indeed, he was convinced that an eventual reunification would not occur by force or violence, but only through discussion. This schism divided families and homes, which was painful for Augustine.

"John Leaned on the Bosom of the Lord"[7]

Augustine sees John as an eagle soaring to great heights, gazing steadily at the light of truth, contemplating the Word of God.[8] From the beginning of the Gospel, John the Evangelist is drawn into the spheres of heaven and earth, in order to speak about the Son of God. Augustine describes John as one who had scaled a mountain, who had reached the summit of peace and contemplated the divinity of the Word. He chose the Gospel of John because this Gospel best illuminates the mystery of Christ, God and man. According to Augustine, the Gospel of John is the most profound Gospel. John wrote about the Word of God and about its eternal origin. From the beginning, Augustine realized the difficulty of the content. He recognized his own limits and took refuge in personal and common prayer to elevate himself to spiritual comprehension. Augustine was touched deeply by the Gospel of John, the beloved disciple who rested upon the bosom of Jesus at the Last Supper. This signified to him that John drank the deeper secrets from the depths of the heart of Jesus.

"Let Us Search Together"[9]

Augustine knew how to speak to the people and developed a dialogical preaching style, which had the tone of a familial conversation. His preaching was intellectually incisive, yet took place in lively interaction with his audience. Because he prepared himself through meditation and prayer and wrote nothing down, he could interact with the faithful and respond immediately to their comments. He sat on his *cathedra* to discuss the text of the Holy Scripture and to be nourished by the faithful according to their capacity, and in turn, he ministered to them from the source from which he himself was nourished.[10] His approach was to inspire interactive and spontaneous conversation, based on structured and thorough preparation. His hearers could not remain unaffected; he involved them directly in this pursuit, inviting them to listen together to the Word of God. He would ask them questions and invite them to look together for solutions. "Let us search together" is a refrain in his homilies. In this way, he developed a lively dialogue of catechesis with the faithful. As an attentive educator, he observed the reactions of his listeners: "For I appear to your eyes, He presides over your consciences. Give me then your ears, Him your hearts, that you may fill both....But lift your hearts to the Lord to be filled."[11] If he saw they did not understand, he would always explain further. He was not afraid to repeat the same idea several times in order to strengthen and deepen the faith.[12]

Preaching is an event in which the life of the Church becomes visible as a place of mutual exchange. The whole people of God is involved; preacher and audience are one. Together they pray that the Holy Spirit might enlighten their hearts. Together they listen to the Word of God, hoping that it may germinate, grow, and bear fruit. Augustine invited his audience to inquire peacefully without quarreling, to listen with their hearts to the divine Word of God, to pray before preaching. As a minister of the Word, Augustine can inspire us toward a spirituality of togetherness through dialogue and prayer.

"LISTEN WITH ME":
A SPIRITUALITY OF TOGETHERNESS

Augustine based his dialogical preaching upon listening together to God's Word in silence. Aware of his own limits, in humility he thought that his way of speaking was unworthy of the subject. Sometimes he acknowledged that he did not understand fully what could be interpreted, or could not present what he understood clearly. He invited the faithful to search together for the explanation of the Gospel: "I say this briefly, until I give a fuller solution: Inquire peacefully, without quarreling, without contention, without altercations, without enmities."[13] Preacher and audience are united as listeners to the eternal Word. In his sermons, Augustine called the faithful to enter with him into the mystery of God's Word. Therefore he invited the faithful, "Listen with me."[14]

"For We Have All One Master, and We Are Fellow Disciples in One School"[15]

Augustine reminds us that the dialogical dimension of human existence has its roots in biblical tradition. God did not create men as isolated creatures, but as relational beings, capable of building relationships and dialogue. Man is created in the image and likeness of God. Through revelation, God has been manifested as the One who listens to and speaks with his people, inviting them into his company. Through Jesus Christ, who is true God and true man, humanity has become testimony of the unique dialogue between God and man. Jesus Christ, who is in fully dialogical unity with his Father, simultaneously lives and gives his life for others. Christ is the fulfillment and fullness of dialogue.

Augustine preached from his heart and the richness of his own faith; the Bible was an inexhaustible resource for him. In addition, he felt united with the faithful to whom he spoke—on the one hand, he stood face-to-face with God, on the other, face-to-face with the faithful. Holy Scripture had a central place in Augustine's life. In the Bible, he sought inspiration for his way of life, his spirituality, his theology, and his pastoral work. As minister of the Word, Augustine wanted to preach to the faithful from that source from which he himself also was nourished.[16] Many times he asked the Lord on behalf of the faithful to explain to them the meaning of the divine Word. Both the preacher and the faithful need a deep and inner relationship with Christ, which leads to a bond of togetherness of both preacher and faithful with Christ.

Augustine's preaching was very biblical. He preached the Bible, through the Bible, and with the Bible. For him, to listen to the Bible was to listen to Christ. In his handbook for study and preaching Scripture, *On Christian Doctrine*, he emphasized the importance of nurturing a deep relationship with the Bible. Studying the Bible leads to an understanding of the will of God and ultimately to real happiness. Augustine had personally discovered and recognized God as the source of the happiness of humanity. To him, the only way to God is Christ, who is the Way, the Truth, and the Life. Reading the Bible can generate and strengthen our love of God and of our neighbor.[17]

Augustine saw each page of the Bible as a revelation of the love of God. In that context, he used the image of the arrow to talk about the Word of God. "You have pierced our hearts with the arrow of your love, and our minds were pierced with the arrows of your words."[18] He discovered the healing and cleansing power of the Word of God. Reading the Bible became a communication, a dialogue, an intimate prayer with God.

Augustine's biblical spirituality can be a source of inspiration for us today. The preacher and the faithful are fellow students in one school. They all have one Teacher. It is Christ who preaches; Christ is the inner Teacher. The human teacher can do his best but it is always Christ who is the true Teacher of the heart.[19]

"Be a Prayer before a Preacher"[20]

"Be a prayer before a preacher." For Augustine, a sacred orator must listen to the Word of God before speaking. If a preacher does not listen to the Word of God within himself, he will preach it in vain to others. The preacher is not just a thinker; he is someone who begins by listening to the voice of the Lord in prayer. In preaching, you bring out your inner self; you pour forth what you have taken in. Augustine prepared himself to preach by prayer and meditation. He emphasized not only his own prayer for the faithful, but also the prayer of the faithful for the preacher: "You may pray for us, that the Lord may grant to us to speak what is suitable, and that you may be found worthy to receive what is suitable."[21] He continually invited his audience to search with him, to pray with him, that the inspiration of the Holy Spirit might lead him to a clear and moving exegesis, that the light of the Holy Spirit might open the hearts of the faithful to understand the preaching, that they might grow spiritually and be brought to eternal salvation.

Following in Augustine's footsteps, Christian spirituality can emphasize not only the prayer of the preacher for the faithful but also the prayer of the faithful for the preacher. Realizing that there are passages in Scripture that are difficult to understand, Christians can invite each other to search together, to pray together so that the inspiration of the Holy Spirit might lead the preacher to a clear and moving exegesis, that the light of the Holy Spirit might open the hearts of the faithful. Augustine reminds us that there is no reason to become discouraged, and he invites us to seek God who is to be found, to seek him who has been found.

For Augustine the preaching of the Divine Word is based upon a prayerful dialogue from heart to heart through listening together to God's Word in silence. The prayerful dialogue with God becomes the spiritual source and strength for the dialogue with men. Christian spirituality is a spirituality of prayer, listening, and speaking with God from heart to heart, preaching for the faithful from heart to heart. Dialogue not only has an intellectual dimension of theological expertise but also an existential dimension of personal engagement through prayer. Dialogue has not only horizontal but also vertical dimensions, from the heart of man to the heart of God. Prayer is the soul of dialogue.[22]

Augustine does not consider prayer a monologue, but a dialogue. God speaks to us through the Holy Scriptures.

Our prayer is an answer to God's Word because his eternal Word precedes us. Man can only prepare a place to receive the Divine Word in his human heart. When we pray, the initiative comes from God because he has created us out of love. He has loved us first. He has searched for us before we sought him. God awaits us, but he does not wait in the same way as men wait. If God is waiting, he waits with endless patience. God has taken the initiative to dialogue with men, not only through words, but also through the language of the heart. We hear God's voice in the intimacy of our hearts. Augustine invites us to pray with the heart, rather than with the lips.

"Longing Is the…Bosom of the Heart"[23]

Augustine called the faithful to pray and to long for God, to deepen and to widen their holy desires. Prayer is about desire and yearning. Desire is the heart of prayer. If someone is without desire, he is mute before God. Desire is always praying. "Longing is the very bosom of the heart. We shall attain, if with all our power we give way to our longing."[24] Therefore the preacher has to encourage his audience. He has to stimulate their desire, so that their faith may be increased and strengthened. Preaching presupposes that the orator meditates, ruminates on the Word of God. He receives the Word of God; he takes it up into his heart so that he can transmit it to others. John reclined upon the breast of the Lord; he received that he might give. In the same way Augustine asked the faithful to open their hearts to his words: "And therefore, dearly beloved, let what has been said, if thought sufficient, be received in a healthful way, as pasture for the holy sheep; and if it is somewhat scanty, let it be ruminated over with ardent desire for more."[25] Longing is related to love. People who love each other, long for each other. Our desire can grow. We can be

11

attracted by truth, by happiness, by justice, by love, by Christ and God. Only those who love and desire can understand this. "You hold out a green twig to a sheep, and you draw it. Nuts are shown to a child, and he is attracted; he is drawn by what he runs to, drawn by loving it, drawn without hurt to the body, drawn by a cord of the heart."[26] The voice of prayer is in the center of the heart. Prayer helps men to make progress on their pilgrimage to the heavenly Jerusalem by strengthening their desire for eternal happiness. The preacher has to encourage the faithful to journey by love as pilgrims, to dwell on high by love, by that love with which we love God.

"That All May Be One"

In *Tractate* 110 Augustine comments on John 17:21, "That all may be one." As elsewhere in his works, here Augustine develops the idea of prayer as a pilgrimage through the dynamic progress of the three virtues: faith, hope, and love. These are gifts of God and are the heart of every prayer. In his commentary on Jesus' desire for unity, Augustine parallels the three phrases of John 17:21. Augustine affirms that it is faith in the Trinity that builds Christian unity, partial in this life, but perfect in the future life. Referring to the verse "that they may be one in us" Augustine explains that the Lord added "in us," "in order that we may know that our being made one in that love of unchanging faithfulness is to be attributed to the grace of God, and not to ourselves."[27] This means that the unity of Christians is built by faith and charity, which are gifts of God. Augustine analyzes a further dynamic progression between verse 21, "That they may be one," and verse 23, "That they may be perfectly one." According to Augustine "to be one" is realized through faith and charity, "to be perfectly one" through vision and hope. Perfect unity will be accomplished in the future coming kingdom of heaven. This is the hope to which the Lord rouses his people. "Listen, and rejoice in hope....Listen, I say, and weigh well to what it is that our hopes are exalted. Jesus Christ is speaking.... Listen, believe, hope, desire what He says."[28]

Through his prayer to the Father at the Last Supper, Christ has taught us to pray. Emphasizing the intimacy of the union between Christ and his members through prayer, Augustine evokes the unity of the whole Christ, in which we love and pray. Head and Body, Head and members, are one Christ. Christ prays for us as priest. He prays for us as the head of the Body of the Church. Our prayer is a participation in the prayer of Christ. As soon as Christ begins to pray, we may understand that we are in him, that we may share our prayer with him. The Body of Christ is praying, the one Church of Christ is praying, the unified Head and members is praying. Christ is the heavenly Teacher, the faithful Counsellor, who exhorts us to ask, to seek, to knock, to pray.[29] Prayer develops our desire and enlarges our hearts until they are capable of containing God's gift of himself. Our prayers are the breezes that fan the flame of our love. For Augustine a praying person is a lover, "one that longs, one that hungers, one that is traveling in this wilderness, and thirsting and panting after the fountain of his eternal home."[30] It was the desire of Christ to identify us with himself. We are all one in Christ, walking the pilgrim way, in the desire of a truly happy life. Prayer is a pilgrimage of the heart.

CHAPTER 2

The Humble Christ

A CHRIST-CENTERED SPIRITUALITY

Christ is central in the preaching of Saint Augustine and his spirituality is a Christ-centered spirituality. Christian spirituality derives its source and existence from a passionate love of Christ. Augustine never separated the Church from Christ. His reflection on the Church takes the person and the works of Christ as the point of departure. One of Augustine's most important tasks in the *Tractates on the Gospel of John* was to make Christians realize that Christ is fully God just as he is fully man, that Christ is the master of humility, and that he is a real example to imitate.

Unus Christus: Deus et Homo
(One Christ, God and Man)

As fully God, Christ is fully man, and yet he is mysteriously one Christ. Augustine's reflections on the union of Word and human being in Christ are not theoretical. He wants to highlight God's unique initiative for human salvation. The Son has not lost his divinity in the incarnation. The Son is equal to the Father and he truly became man. The unity of divinity and humanity in the one person of Christ is the spiritual source of unity between God and man and among men. Augustine developed this idea extensively

15

in his *Confessions*. According to him, you do not have to ascend to heaven to look for the eternal Word; you have to see that the eternal Word has come down to find us.[1] If we want to live in truth, then we have to grow, but we cannot grow without humility because we are imperfect. If you recognize God in Christ, you will see Christ lying at your feet. Throw yourself down into the depths. As he rises, you will also rise. Commenting on the Gospel of Saint John, Augustine repeats that Jesus takes us down to earth, because that is the only way to heaven.

Christus Redemptor (Christ the Redeemer)

Augustine uses many expressions to clarify the link between incarnation and redemption. The Word of God became man to free humankind from sin. He is the unique Mediator through whom alone humanity can be saved. Christ has become the creator and re-creator, the maker and re-maker. Augustine frequently refers to the cross as the central symbol of the redemption of Christ. The wood of Noah's Ark refers to the wood of the cross on which the Life of the World was fastened. Moses striking the rock at Meribah with his staff symbolizes Christ as Rock. Augustine also connects the cross with the incarnation. In *Tractate* 2, he compares the cross to a ship. By the wood of the cross, we may cross the sea. We cannot cross over the sea to the homeland unless the wood carries us. Therefore, the Lord walked on the sea, that he might show that there is a way on the sea. "For no one can cross the sea of this world unless borne by the cross of Christ."[2] The faithful have to cling with confidence to the cross that brings us all safely over the sea to the homeland.

According to Augustine, the spiritual value of the cross is very important. Wounded by a spear, Christ the physician cured our wounds by enduring his wounds. He healed us of eternal death when he died a temporal death. The palm branches that greeted Christ during his entry into Jerusalem symbolize praise, signifying victory. The Lord overcame death by dying, and by the cross he triumphed over the devil, the prince of death. By his death on the cross, he brought eternal life. The wooden cross is a *cathedra* of the Master who was teaching pardon and humility. By the death on the cross, Christ poured out his blood for the remission of sins.

In *Tractates* 55–111, Augustine comments on the discourses of Jesus during the Last Supper (John 13—17), describing Jesus as Mediator and Conciliator between God and man to redeem humankind from death. Christ is the reconciling Mediator who came to take away the separating wall, which is sin. The revelation of Christ as Savior, Redeemer, and Mediator is a real appeal to unity. "As a teacher, He brought truth; as a deliverer, He brought gentleness; as a protector, He brought righteousness."[3] The redemption and mediation of Christ is not limited to the reconciliation of people with God, but extends to the realization of the unity of humankind. Christ is the author and the center of the unity between men.

Christus Pastor (Christ the Shepherd)

Commenting on chapter 10 of the Gospel of John, Augustine affirms that there is only one Shepherd, Christ. Yet Augustine frequently asks how it is possible that Jesus speaks about one Shepherd when there are many shepherds. Augustine reflects on this apparent contradiction by saying that all those shepherds are members of the one Shepherd. It is Christ who acts through their ministry and through this he guides the unity of baptism and the Church. The voice of the Shepherd is a true voice; it is the very voice of salvation. The Shepherd knows and calls his own sheep by name and leads them to eternal life. Christ is the Shepherd in the sheepfold, which is the Church. Christ is also the Gate to the sheepfold—the Father—for there is no way by which one may come to the Father except through him. Christ is the true and good Shepherd and as such is a model for all shepherds.

Augustine refers to the distinction between shepherds and hired hands. Hired hands do not seek God, but rather profits and honors for themselves. The shepherd is called to proclaim the true Christ, and not himself. He is called to seek Christ's glory, not his own. He has to exercise the ministry of humility. Christ the Lord is a lowly door, and one who enters through this door, must lower himself that he may enter unharmed.

Not only are the ministers of the Lord good bishops and clerics, but all those who serve Christ by living well, by giving alms, by preaching his name, including the head of a family who owes its members paternal affection. Those who admonish for Christ's sake, teach, encourage, correct, discipline, and those who offer bread to the hungry out of mercy rather than display, are ministers. In this way, not only ministers—in the strict sense of the word—but everyone in his or her own house "will be filling an ecclesiastical and kind of episcopal office,"[4] serving Christ.

Lest the minister consider the sheep his own, Augustine emphasizes that the minister is not a master, but a servant. The sheep do not belong to him, but to Christ. The One Shepherd is Christ in the heart of everyone. Those who feed Christ's sheep must not be lovers of themselves, but lovers of Christ, always keeping in mind that the sheep are not theirs but Christ's. Let it be the duty of love to feed the Lord's flock. "Let us, then, love not ourselves, but Him; and in feeding His sheep, let us be seeking the things which are His, not the things which are our own...lest they feed them as if they were their own, and not His, and wish to make their own gain of them, as 'lovers of money'; or to domineer over them, as 'boastful'; or to glory in the honors which they receive at their hands, as 'proud'."[5]

Christus Via et Patria
(Christ the Way and the Homeland)

Augustine links the themes of the way and the homeland —*Via et Patria*—when he speaks about Christ. More than just an image, it gives Augustine the opportunity to preach on the humanity and the divinity of the one Christ.

In using the images of the way and the homeland, Augustine reflects deeply on this duality. The homeland of man is God. The way to this homeland is Christ. This is a reference to the idea of the Pilgrim Church, a concept that would be developed by the Second Vatican Council. Through the mystery of incarnation, Christ is the only way that leads to God. There is no other way to the divinity of Christ than through his humanity. His divinity is where we are going; his humanity is the way by which we are going. "He is the door to the Father, for there is no way of approach to the Father but by Him. 'For there is one God and one Mediator between God and men, the man Christ Jesus.'"[6]

Christ's example is not limited to a few acts but embraces the whole incarnation. Everything that Jesus has said and done is a lesson for us, even his death on the cross. His example is a way of suffering and self-emptying love. The example of Christ's earthly life is the starting point for us to pass through his humanity to reach his divinity. By his humanity, we can reach the divinity. "You come to Christ by Christ. How by Christ to Christ? By Christ the man, to Christ God; by the Word made flesh, to the Word which in the beginning was God with God."[7]

Christ is not only the way; he is also the destination. He is our perfection. The historical acts of Christ are our way because his life on earth shows us how to live by imitating him and because they establish the teachings of our faith, by which we move above to the eternal vision. Augustine describes the life of humanity as a journey on a ship in the sea. Augustine knew very well the dangers of the sea both from his own experience and from the contact with the fishermen that he met by the sea. The sea represents human life, full of dangers, while the ship refers to the means that Christ puts at our disposal from pure mercy. When the storm rages, one must cling to Christ.

> Therefore, my brethren, I would desire to have impressed this upon your hearts: if you wish to live in a pious and Christian manner, cling to Christ according to that which He became for us, that you may arrive at Him according to that which is, and according to that which was. He approached, that for us He might become this; because He became that for us, on which the weak may be borne, and cross the sea of this world and reach their native country; where there will be no need of a ship, for no sea is crossed.[8]

There is no way by which man can cross over to the homeland unless he is carried by the ship, by the wood, by the cross of Christ. Abiding with the Father, Christ, who is the Truth and the Life, clothed himself with flesh and became the Way. With his flesh and his cross, Christ is a unique ship to cross the sea to the homeland. One can approach the mystery of the incarnation and the death of Christ with faith. Through faith, man trusts himself to the cross that will bring him to the homeland. This faith requires humility and leads to humility, the humility of Christ.

Augustine wants to arouse longing in the hearts of the faithful, longing for a heavenly life. He describes the heavenly life as the joy of being with Christ, a feast day that lasts through eternity, a festival, pure joy without end, eternity without blemish, serenity without a cloud.

With the words "Love with me," Augustine invites the faithful to walk along the way and to desire the joy and peace of the homeland: "I beseech you, love with me, by believing run with me: let us long for our home above, let us pant for our home above, let us feel that we are strangers here….You shall come to the fountain….You will see that very light….I feel that your affections are being lifted up with me to the things that are above."[9]

CHRIST, THE WOUNDED HEALER

Christus Medicus (Christ the Physician)

Augustine uses the theme of *Christus medicus* in his theology of sin and redemption.[10] By the medicine of his humility, Christ, the Divine Physician, heals mankind from the wound of pride. Augustine uses a wide range of images to highlight the therapeutic action of Christ. He compares Christ to a physician who cures ailing eyes with salve. Christ applied stinging salves, the commandments of justice and love on the eyes of our hearts.[11] He removed the source of all sins— pride—with the divine medicine of his humility. The "Word made flesh" became medicine for us. He is the Universal Physician, the Divine Healer of mankind's spiritual diseases.

For Augustine, the whole history of the incarnation of Christ is medicinal. The incarnation is medicine for the blindness of man. By his nativity, Christ made a salve to cleanse the eyes of our heart, that we might be able to see his majesty through his lowliness. The incarnation is a medicinal act to heal the deepest part of man, to transform the proud and blind heart into humility. "[In order] that the cause of all diseases might be cured, namely, pride, the Son of God came down and was made low."[12]

This healing is a continuous process and goes further into the final goal of faith. When Jesus speaks and acts, man can see with the eyes of the faithful heart through Christ man to Christ God, through the Son of Man to the Son of God, the eternal Word. The humanity of Christ attracts us. As a child is attracted by his mother's milk, so man is attracted by the humanity of Christ. Man is attracted by what is accessible. Man can drink milk that he may be nourished, that he may be strong enough for solid food, to advance in the faith of Christ and to grasp the divinity of Christ.[13] The humanity of the humble Christ nourishes us, as if he were giving milk to little ones, so that we may arrive at the solid food of the immutable truth, the divinity of Christ. The internal transformation and the conversion of the heart does not happen automatically. Man can only be healed by responding to Christ with receptiveness and availability, and to do this, it is necessary to acknowledge one's own spiritual illness.

While Augustine describes the pedagogical and exemplary aspects of the medical activity of Christ in the incarnation, he highlights the meaning in Christ's death on the cross. The suffering and the death of Christ on the cross constitute medicine that heals all wounds inflicted by sin. Jesus Christ is the only Physician who can heal the wounds of the soul. Christ is the wounded Healer. He was beaten, whipped, smeared with spittle, crowned with thorns, hung upon a cross, deprived of life, wounded by a spear, taken down from the cross, and interred in a tomb. As the complete Physician, he cured our wounds while enduring his own. He healed us from eternal death. The death of Christ is a manifestation of the mercy of Christ because he was free from sin. He did not merit suffering and death, but he suffered and died for our sake.[14]

Augustine emphasizes that it is not just one particular moment in the life of Christ that heals man. The whole life of the incarnate Word of God, what he has said, what he has done, his death and resurrection, have illustrated the role of the merciful Lord as *Christus medicus*. Christ is the wounded Healer. All humans need his healing power because of their weakness. All Christians are called to pray to the merciful Lord that he might heal the wounds of the past.

The Pierced Side of Christ on the Cross

According to Augustine, the value of the cross is very important. Wounded by a spear, Christ the Physician cured our wounds while enduring his own wounds. He healed us of eternal death in dying a temporal death. The healing principle, the medicine, is the cross, while the physician is the Crucified.

By making the sign of the cross, a sign of faith, Christians can encourage each other to give witness of their faith in a secularized world. They sign themselves with the name of God the Father, the Son, and the Spirit. Those who make this sign want to express that they are children of the Father, brothers and sisters of the Son, and houses of the Holy Spirit.

Augustine describes the moment when the soldier opened Christ's side, and immediately there came out blood and water. Augustine interprets this piercing as the opening of the door of life. From Christ's pierced side the sacraments flowed.[15] Augustine explains that blood refers to the remission of sins: "Water it is that makes up the health-giving cup, and supplies at once the laver of baptism and water for drinking."[16] The death of Christ is the medicine for our diseases.

When Augustine speaks about the healing activity of Christ, he is not only referring to the earthly Jesus but to the "whole Christ," the *Christus Totus*. Augustine emphasized the intimate bond between Christ and Christians, the Head and the Body. To describe this intimate bond, Augustine developed his thought on the "whole Christ," the mystery of Christ and his Church. Life, suffering, and resurrection can only be understood from the life, suffering, and resurrection of Christ. The "whole Christ" exercises the healing function in different ways, through pastoral ministry, reading and preaching the Bible, the ministry of the sacraments.

According to Augustine, the Church must be a place where the wounded are healed, just like the travelers' inn in the parable of the good Samaritan.[17] The true pastors of the Church are driven by a merciful love that heals wounds. All Christians are called to imitate the merciful Lord who heals the wounds of the past.

The cry of the dying Christ on the cross becomes the cry of Christ for the unity of his Body, which is the Church. Augustine, who felt the pain of a divided Church, called the faithful to imitate the humble Christ. Christ came to show the way of humility and to make himself the very Way of humility. We are cleansed by the lowliness and humility of Christ.[18]

CHRISTUS HUMILIS: CHRIST, THE TEACHER OF HUMILITY

According to Augustine, man's pilgrimage to the heavenly Jerusalem comes by imitating the humble Christ. The humility of Christ is an essential aspect of Augustine's spirituality. Christ is the humble Physician who came to heal the wounds caused by pride with the medicine of humility. He is the master of humility. "We have learned, brethren, humility from the Highest; let us, as humble, do to one another what He, the Highest, did in His humility. Great is the commendation we have here of humility."[19]

Christus humilis (the humble Christ) is a characteristic theme of the spirituality of Saint Augustine.[20] First, Christ's humility heals by contrast. God creates with power and saves with humility. "We find a strong and a weak Jesus…. The strength of Christ created you, the weakness of Christ created you anew….He fashioned us by His strength, He sought us by his weakness."[21] Augustine describes the redemptive work of Christ with medical images of cleansing, purifying, and healing. The humble physician works radically and searches for the cause and fountainhead of all diseases, pride. Therefore, in order that pride might be healed, the Son of God became humble. Christ's humility is the antidote to human pride.

We can also consider the humility of Christ in his role as Mediator between God and man. The mediation of Christ culminates in the joining of humanity to the divinity in Christ's person. As Mediator between God and man, he reconciles through humility all that divides God and humanity. Augustine describes the death of Christ on the cross as the culmination of the humble pathway to God. The humility of Christ carries the promise of our redemption. Through his humility, the eternal God descends to our mortality in order to invite our ascent to immortality.

The humility of Christ is also a *kenosis*, a self-emptying love. Augustine was inspired by the second chapter of the Letter of the apostle Paul to the Philippians (2:6–11), in which Christ is portrayed as humble and self-emptying. Inspired by this christological hymn, Augustine highlights the humility of Christ's *kenosis*, and the humble act of self-emptying love from the incarnation to the passion. Augustine tries to understand why God chose such an extreme means as death on a cross. Christ did not seek his own glory but the glory of the Father, who exalted him above all. Christ's descent into humanity, into death, into the grave, becomes the road to ascent. His death is the completion of the *kenosis* first revealed in the Word made flesh. The abasement of Christ in the form of a servant is the road of humility and exaltation. The Son became man in time, he received the form of a servant, he delivered his life in obedience to the Father, he did not seek his own glory, but the glory of the Father, and he has been exalted. There is an intrinsic connection between humiliation and exaltation. The death that is the supreme manifestation of the humiliation of the Son becomes victory due to his exaltation. In his obedience to the cross, the humiliated Christ reveals the glory and the divine power inside his self-emptying act.

In *Tractate* 4, Augustine describes the progressive humiliation of Christ from the incarnation through the different moments of his life until death on the cross. The humility of Christ is not only one moment or one act, but it is a permanent progression into self-emptying love. The incarnation is the basis and the foundation for the ongoing process of the humiliation of Christ. In his homilies, Augustine repeats that the humbled Son has become the model for humility, the source of Christian behavior. More particularly, he sees the gesture of humility through foot washing as an act of fraternal love. The humility of Christ is really the fundamental virtue of Christian life. The imitation of the humble Christ finds its source in the mystery of self-emptying love. The mystery of self-emptying love through humility, obedience, and death is anchored in the merciful plan of the Father. Christ is the center and source of

Christian humility ever since his actualization of the merciful plan of divine goodness.

Augustine repeats that the Son of God came down and became humble to cure us with his own humility, in order that the cause of all diseases—pride—might be healed. Humility is the only medicine that can heal humanity. By death on the cross, Christ calls us to imitate him in humility that eliminates the death in which we find ourselves.

Augustine comments on the foot washing in five *Tractates* (55–59). He develops a profound meditation on the humility of Christ when the Lord washes the feet of the apostles at the Last Supper. He analyzes the allegorical sense of the preparatory gestures of Christ before the foot washing. Though he was in the form of God, Christ emptied himself. Taking the form of a servant, he tied a towel around himself. He put water in a basin with which he might wash the feet of his disciples, with which he might wash the uncleanness of sins. At his crucifixion, he was stripped of his garments; and when he was dead, he was wrapped in linens. His whole passion is our healing.

According to Augustine, these gestures refer to the mystery of the incarnation of Christ and his work of purification. This gesture is not only a sign, but also an example from which Augustine derives a moral and a spiritual interpretation. According to Augustine, the Lord refers to baptism when he says that even the man who has bathed needs to wash his feet. By baptism a man is wholly washed, because baptism cleans all sins. Yet man continues to walk, he steps on the ground and dust sticks to his feet. This means that even after baptism, man continues to experience sin. Therefore, Christ who intercedes for us daily, washes our feet for us. No matter how much progress we have made in the practice of justice, we know that we are not without sin. Christ repeatedly washes our sins away by interceding for us when we pray to the Father in heaven to forgive us our debts as we forgive our debtors. The forgiveness symbolized in foot washing takes place after baptism and needs to be done continually for the remission of sins. Augustine highlights the community aspect of the prayer of the Lord when he concludes, "Let us therefore forgive one another his faults, and pray for one another's faults, and thus in a manner be washing one another's feet. It is our part, by His grace, to be supplying the service of love and humility."[22] The humility of Christ unifies mankind and establishes community. "If pride caused diversities of tongues, Christ's humility has united these diversities in one."[23]

Augustine wants to clarify that Christ's whole passion is our cleansing and that we are called to follow the humility of the Redeemer. Augustine refers to the reaction of Peter, who trembled in fear when he saw that Jesus wanted to wash his feet. Terrified by the depth of the Lord's deed, Peter did not wish to see the humbled Christ down at his feet; he could not bear it. According to Augustine, the gesture of foot washing refers to the mystery of the incarnation of Christ and his work of purification. This gesture is not only a sign, but also an example. Augustine repeats that Jesus came to teach humility. For Augustine, humility, based on Christ's humility, is really the fundamental virtue of Christian life.

Augustine refers to people who think that they have to climb up a mountain to be near to God, but they forget that God is closest to the humble man. In his sermons, Augustine calls Christians to come down to the lowness, because there they will reach the Highest. He invites the faithful to imitate Christ, the Teacher of humility, the model for humility. The humble Christ is an example to follow on the road of humility.

CHAPTER 3

Through the Guidance of the Holy Spirit

The third spiritual theme is the Holy Spirit as the principle of unity. The road to harmony is through the guidance of the Holy Spirit. Christian unity is a gift of the Holy Spirit. The Church is the Body of Christ and the Holy Spirit is the soul of the Church. The Holy Spirit is the spirit of unity, the bond of love.

THE SPIRIT AS GIFT TO AND SOUL OF THE CHURCH

Augustine not only describes the role of the Spirit in the Trinity as charity that unites the Father and the Son, but also his relation and activity toward human beings. The love of God does not stay locked up within God but pours forth in our hearts by the fervor of the Spirit. Augustine describes the Holy Spirit as the gift of God, "the greatest gift that God can give."[1]

Augustine uses the image of the Holy Spirit as soul of the Church in order to explain the relationship between the Holy Spirit and unity. The love of the Holy Spirit enlivens the Body of Christ. The Spirit is not only at the origin of the Church, the Spirit is the soul and life itself of the Church.

Therefore, Augustine compares the Holy Spirit with the human soul, which as principle puts the whole body in motion. By the one Spirit, the members of Christ's Body are enlivened.[2] Saint Augustine can inspire us here. What the soul is to the human body, the Holy Spirit is to the Body of Christ, the Church. The Holy Spirit is the bond of unity.

In his work on the Trinity, Augustine writes, "many gifts, which are proper to each, are divided in common to all the members of Christ by the Gift, which is the Holy Spirit. For each severally has not all, but some have these and some have those; although all have the Gift itself by which that which is proper to each is divided by Him, i.e. the Holy Spirit."[3] In his commentaries on the psalms, Augustine explains that the Holy Spirit distributed his gifts and made some apostles, others prophets, pastors, or doctors. In this way, the Holy Spirit wanted to increase the beauty of his house. No one should lament that he has not received a gift that another received, or be jealous of someone else's gift.[4] In *Tractate* 32, Augustine invites the faithful to take away envy, because jealousy separates and right reason unites. Referring to the charisms mentioned by Saint Paul in the First Letter to the Corinthians, Augustine reflects on the charismatic side of the Church. In the Body of Christ, there is a plurality of gifts of the Holy Spirit or charisms such as wisdom, knowledge, prophecy, discerning of spirits, the gift of healing. This plurality of gifts does not break the unity of the Church because the same Spirit distributes all these gifts. Augustine not only refers to a plurality of gifts given by the Holy Spirit, but also mentions the importance of regional, linguistic, and liturgical diversity. Through this plurality, Christians are united by one Spirit in one Body, whose Head is Christ.

THE SPIRIT AS AGENT OF
UNITY AND RECONCILIATION

One of the central benefits of the Holy Spirit is his unifying activity. The Holy Spirit is the unifying link of love
between the Father and the Son. According to Augustine,
the Holy Spirit is principle of communion and unity. The
Holy Spirit not only represents the unity of the Father and
the Son, but also wants us to join with the Father and the
Son through his love as well.

The Holy Spirit is *communio*, communion of love. In
and through the Holy Spirit, God is close to humankind in
his love. The Holy Spirit wants to bond people with one
another. He wants to found a community of love among
men. The Holy Spirit calls us to imitate God's communion of
unity and love. To be a Christian is to become communion.
To believe in the Holy Spirit as communion is not optional
or open-ended. As an example, Augustine refers to the first
Christian community in Jerusalem. The Holy Spirit has been
given to the apostles, to the first community in Jerusalem, to
the Church. After the Holy Spirit was received, they were
brought into one group by the very love and fervor of the
Spirit, and began in the very unity of fellowship to sell all
their possessions so that the proceeds might be distributed
to each one as needed. They had one soul and one heart.
Through love, many souls are one soul, and many hearts are
one heart, by the power of the Holy Spirit. By the one Spirit,
the members of Christ's Body are enlivened. The Spirit that
gives life produces living members.[5] Through his love, the
Holy Spirit unifies the Church.

The Spirit is the Gift who enables us to be in communion with God and with one another. The variety of
tongues given by the Spirit refers to the unity of the Church.
Augustine describes the Holy Spirit as the agent of unity

and reconciliation in the communion of the Church. The Holy Spirit empowers the Church to seek for and to live in unity through love and reconciliation.[6]

In his sermons and in his work *The City of God*, Augustine describes Babel as the city built on self-love, while Jerusalem—the City of God—is the city built on the love of God.[7] Augustine compares two types of unity: the unity of Babel and the unity of Pentecost, unity according to the flesh and unity according to the Spirit.[8] The unity of Babel is a human unity, decided by human beings and with the aim of the glory of human beings. In Babel, everyone places himself at the center, with the consequence that words only divide and separate. People no longer understand one another. The unity of Pentecost speaks of the apostles who do not raise a monument to themselves but to God. De-centered from themselves, they are re-centered on God. They accept God as the center of their lives.

The Second Vatican Council affirmed that the Church is a communion of believers in Jesus Christ and that the Holy Spirit is the principle of unity of the Church.[9] On the day of Pentecost "was foreshadowed the union of all peoples…a church which speaks every language, understands and embraces all tongues in charity, and thus overcomes the dispersion of Babel."[10] The Spirit is the agent of unity and actualizer of diversity in Church-*communio*. One must make the distinction between differences that are divisive and differences that are not Church-dividing. The Spirit supports diversity within a fundamental unity and togetherness.

THE SPIRIT AS LOVE

Augustine sees the Holy Spirit as the bond of love within the Trinity, within the world, and between the world and God. He emphasizes the link between intra-Trinitarian communion and ecclesial communion. Reflecting on the unifying activity of the Spirit within the Trinity, Augustine affirms that the Holy Spirit gathers the Church into unity, inflames us with love of God and neighbor, brings fire and fervor to love. Augustine calls the Spirit the Source of Love and the Fountain of Charity. According to Augustine, these titles remind us that charity emanates from the Spirit and is implanted in our hearts.[11]

Referring to Saint Paul (Rom 5:5), "God's love has been poured into our hearts through the Holy Spirit that has been given to us," Augustine calls the gift of the Holy Spirit our greatest benefit. To Augustine it was clear that unity can be effected only by the love poured out by the Holy Spirit, the love by which we become lovers for God. The Spirit acts not through opposition but through togetherness. The Spirit is the bond of union, the love at the root of Christian love.

The Spirit who unites the Father and the Son as the bond of love and peace, can unify with the same love many hearts to the Body of Christ. The love poured forth through the Holy Spirit is not only the charity by which we love God, but also the charity by which we love our neighbor, as the union of soul and heart has been realized through the Holy Spirit of Pentecost. Augustine suggests that the Holy Spirit has been given visibly twice, on the eve of Easter and on the morning of Pentecost, to manifest that the two commandments come from the Holy Spirit.[12] The two commandments, the love of God and the love of neighbor, cannot be separated but are linked together. There is one love because love comes from God. Love has its source in the Holy Spirit. There is one love and there are two commandments. There is one Spirit and there are two gifts.

Charity is true life. If one does not have charity, he does not have the Holy Spirit; if one's body is without spirit, his soul is dead. One can have great faith, but without love, there is no benefit. Faith is not just theoretical or intellectual. Faith loves Christ and clings to Christ. Whoever believes passes from death to life, from injustice to justice, from pride to humility, from hatred to charity.

Here Augustine compares the activity of the Spirit in the Body of Christ and the spirit or the soul in human nature, for the Spirit only produces living members, which it has found in the body that the Spirit itself enlivens. As the human body is enlivened by his spirit, the Body of Christ, which is the Church, is enlivened by the divine life of the Spirit of the Father and the Son. The Body of Christ can only live from the Spirit of Christ. The love that has been given by the Holy Spirit produces the unity of the Body of Christ. Augustine invites the faithful not only to eat the flesh of Christ and drink the blood of Christ in the sacrament, but to eat and to drink in order to participate in the Spirit, that they may abide as members in the Body of the Lord, that they may be enlivened by his Spirit.[13]

Holy Scripture testifies that the Holy Spirit is not only the source of love but is, rather, Love itself. The Spirit as Love is not an abstract idea, but he is the substantial love of the Father and the Son. The Spirit is the power of God's love, which has been poured forth in our hearts. Therefore, the Spirit says something not only about God but also about us. God is Spirit and the Spirit is the gift of God in us. In that sense, the Spirit has to do with spirituality, which means the attitude of our own spirit. We must let the Spirit of God form our minds. Charity enables humankind to approach God and to become one soul and one heart. This unifying work is the activity of the Holy Spirit.

Augustine intended to touch the human heart with a rich visual language of symbols. Referring to the Holy Spirit, Augustine evokes different biblical symbols such as the dove, tongues of fire, and the source of living water. The word *symbol* comes from the Greek and means "connecting, unifying." Symbols have a binding value; they can bring people together. The Church has a visible aspect, derived from the incarnation, and an invisible aspect, derived from the presence of the Spirit. Christian spirituality must revitalize the symbols of the Spirit in order to express this mysterious, invisible side of the Church.

In *Tractate* 6, Augustine describes the symbolic teachings of the Holy Spirit by means of his two visible manifestations, in the dove at the baptism of Jesus and in the tongues of fire at Pentecost.

Augustine felt that the Holy Spirit is the divine source of ardor in the Church and among Christians. On the one hand, the Holy Spirit is parted in different tongues, which represent the nations to which the disciples were sent. On the other, the Holy Spirit is united in the dove. "In the dove the unity, in the tongues the community of the nations."[14] Fire is the transforming energy of the actions of the Holy Spirit. Fire is something fascinating. People like to look at flames. People gathered around a fire never look at each other, but they watch the flames. Fire brings people together without words. Fire creates enthusiasm and warms the human heart.

Augustine also speaks about the dove who groans and moans. The Holy Spirit wanted to be shown in the form of a dove. Augustine explains that this is not strange, referring to the Apostle Paul: "the Spirit himself intercedes for us with unspeakable moanings."[15]

> Now if the dove's note is a moaning, as we all know it to be, and doves moan in love....[The dove] moans because he makes us to moan....He gives us to know that we are sojourners in a foreign

land....But he who knows that he is in the pressure of this mortal life, a pilgrim absent from the Lord, that he does not yet possess that perpetual blessedness which is promised to us....he, I say who knows this does moan....It was the Spirit that taught him to moan, he has learned it from the dove.[16]

The groaning of the Spirit encloses and embraces all prayers, sufferings, and praises. In this sense, the Spirit can be called the source of all our prayers. By the energizing power of the Holy Spirit, Christians are able to pray and to worship God. One can also refer to the end of the flood, when a dove released by Noah returns with a fresh olive branch in its beak as a sign that the earth was again habitable. This symbol can be found in early Christian catacombs, symbolizing the resurrection. Currently it is used as a sign of peace.

Another symbol that Augustine uses is the Spirit as the Source of Love and the Fountain of Charity. The ineffable mystery of the Holy Spirit becomes visible in the image of the well and of water. Man's spiritual thirst cries out for the Holy Spirit. The Lord cries out that we should come and drink if we thirst within. When we drink, rivers of living water shall flow out of us. The Spirit is the fountain that flows from Christ's wounded body. It is from Christ's open heart that the waters flow, fountains of living water.

In his commentary on the woman caught in adultery, Augustine refers to the Law that was written by the finger of God.[17] Augustine regularly speaks of the Spirit of God as the finger of God who writes the new law not on stone tablets, but on tablets of living flesh, on the tablets of our hearts. When Thomas reached out his hand and put it in the side of Christ, Augustine comments, "He saw and touched the man, and acknowledged the God whom he nei-ther saw nor touched."[18] Warning against carnal belief, Augustine invites us to reflect on the spiritual touch of faith. Faith grows through this spiritual touch and contact. Men believe when they are touched spiritually, when they touch the Spirit and are touched by the Spirit.

Spirit means wind, breath, respiration. When Jesus appeared to his disciples, he breathed on them and said, "Receive the Holy Spirit." The breath of the Holy Spirit is as a new creation, a true resurrection. Jesus breathed his Spirit to restore humanity. The promise of the Paraclete in the dis-course after the Last Supper gives Augustine occasion to reflect on the transformation of the disciples and the faithful from carnal to spiritual through the Holy Spirit.[19] Knowing the disciples would be sad after his death, Jesus promises to send the Spirit as Comforter. The Spirit will spread himself in their hearts through his charity. They will possess the Trinity in their hearts, and they will bear witness.[20]

The descent of the Holy Spirit results in a sudden and extraordinary transformation. From being carnal, they become spiritual by the charity that has been poured forth in their hearts by the gift of the Holy Spirit. They receive with love the testimony that the Holy Spirit bears about Christ. They believe in truth, "without constraint, with firmness, constancy, and fortitude."[21] By pouring out love in the hearts of believers and by making them spiritual, the Spirit revealed to them how the Son, whom they only knew before accord-ing to the flesh, was equal to the Father. The love that has been poured forth in their hearts makes them very strong witnesses to Christ. By freeing them from fear, by making them capable of enduring everything, the love of the Holy Spirit makes them martyrs—witnesses—to proclaim with confident assurance the resurrection of Christ "they would endure the hardships of all kinds of persecution, and, set aglow at that divine fire, lose none of their warmth in the love of preaching."[22]

Augustine considers Peter the major exemplar of this spiritual transformation. Terrified by the maidservant's questioning, he was unable to testify truthfully and denied the one whom he had loved. When the Holy Spirit was infused into him by an abundance of grace, he was so inflamed that his once-cold breast turned to witnessing to Christ. "When he really received the gift of the Holy Spirit, he preached Him whom he had denied; and whom he had been afraid to confess, he had no fear now in openly pro-claiming….He preached Christ even to the death, whom, in his fear of death, he had previously denied."[23] The Spirit makes men spiritual, giving them a new attitude. The Spirit himself teaches believers, as far as each one can apprehend spiritual things, and each one is capable of growing in desire.

Augustine exhorts the faithful to advance in the love that is poured forth in their hearts by the Holy Spirit in order that, "fervent in spirit, and loving spiritual things, you may be able…by the inward eyesight and hearing, to become acquainted with that spiritual light and that spiritual word which carnal men are unable to bear."[24] The Holy Spirit will guide them; he will teach them all truth. Augustine expresses the hope that they may know what the Lord is doing, that they may be the Lord's friends, associated with his friendship. "Let us be not servants, but sons [of God]: that…we may as servants have the power not to be servants; servants, indeed, with that clean fear which distinguishes the servant that enters into the joy of his lord."[25]

The Holy Spirit was sent to the disciples to teach them all the truth, which they were unable to bear at the time he spoke to them. He reserves his fullness for us until another life, when we shall attain the fullness of knowledge. We do not have full knowledge in this life, but the Lord made us a promise through the love of the Spirit when he said, "He will teach you all truth," and "will guide you unto all truth."[26] The promise of the Lord surpasses our human understanding on earth that will only find its fulfillment in the heavenly homeland. "For in such a way will the Holy Spirit teach you all truth, when He shall shed abroad that love ever more and more largely in your hearts."[27]

CHAPTER 4

The Pilgrim Church

Saint Augustine was a promoter of the unity of the Church, working tirelessly with all possible means to achieve it: travel, debates, councils, preaching, writings, and so on. Saint Augustine preached with a strong passion for Christ and the Church. Although he never wrote a systematic work on the Church, the theme of the Church is present in many of his writings. Augustine's concept of the Church is very complex, yet coherent.

For Augustine the Church is founded in the Holy Trinity. The Church is the Body of Christ, enlivened by the Holy Spirit that has been poured forth in human hearts. The Second Vatican Council rediscovered images of the Church from the patristic era as the Body of Christ, enlivened by the Holy Spirit and as sacrament, sign, and instrument of unity. Deeper reflection reveals that these images are based upon the understanding of the Church as *communio.*

"I HAVE NO OTHER HANDS THAN YOURS…"

A Spirituality of the "Whole Christ"

The Church is not a static reality, but a dynamic movement. The Church is primarily community, in a living, interpersonal relationship with Jesus Christ. In Augustine's thought, there is a very strong unity between Christ and the Church. The profound unity between Christ and the Church is expressed in the well-known doctrine of *Totus Christus*, the "whole Christ." Referring to Saint Paul, Augustine speaks about the whole Christ. As the different parts of a human body make up one person, so the historical Jesus is one with all who believe in him, the whole Christ. The union between the Head and the Body, between Christ and the Church, is so close and intimate that together they form only one organism. There is a deep connection between Christ, the Head, and the faithful, his Body. The whole Christ embraces Head and Body, of which we are the members. Head and Body form the Church.

We can only understand the life, suffering, and resurrection of the Church from the life, suffering, and resurrection of Christ, the Head of the Body that is the Church. The bond between Christ and the Church is so intimate that nothing can dissolve it. The consequences of this intimate union go very deep. Ascended into heaven, Christ continues to live, pray, travel, and suffer in his members who are on earth, Christ in the Church, the Church in Christ. Christ lives, works, and grows in us. Christ still labors and hungers in us. Christ continues to suffer in everyone who belongs to him. Christ still dies in us.[1] The Easter of Christ is also our Easter. We rise in Christ. Christ rises within us. The Church is active in Christ and Christ in the Church, the Body in the Head and the Head in the Body. When we speak, Christ continues to speak in this world. We pray in Christ and he prays in us. He is in us and we are in him. Augustine develops the same idea with regard to the apostolic task of the Church. Christ is working through the ministers of the flock.[2] Christ proclaims himself in the prophets and his disciples.

The Church is a community of faith and love, founded on Christ, the living community of believers in which God lives as in his temple, the diversely composed people of God, including all his members. Augustine feels a passion for Christ and for his Church, animated by the Holy Spirit. The Church is animated and quickened by the Spirit of Christ. One of the central benefits of the Holy Spirit is its unifying activity. The Spirit, who unites the Father and the Son as the bond of love and peace, can unify with the same love so many hearts and the Body of Christ.[3]

This life-relationship of the Church as the *"whole Christ"* can be seen in the impressive crucifix that hangs in the Grail Chapel of the Monsalvaet camp house founded by the Flemish Catholic Student Action in Westouter, West Flanders.[4] This image of Christ reminds us that Christianity is not just about virtues, but also about the one who bears these virtues, Jesus Christ. Around this cross, there is an old story, dating back to final days of the Second World War. While removing debris, an American soldier found a large damaged image of the crucified Christ. As much as he searched, he could not find the arms. Tired of searching, he sat down and looked at the crucifix, almost with pity. People passed, Germans, old women, children in rags, who were depressed, anxious, even maimed. He dared not look at them. He thought to himself, do they have to go on living this way, as ghosts and wrecks amidst ruins? Who would ever love and heal them? Who would ever repair their homes? As he kept his eyes fixed on the helpless Christ, he saw the lips of the Crucified One moving and heard him say, "I have no hands but yours…." This is a core truth: Christ knows firsthand how people suffer and need help. Christ calls people in his name, to transform the evil into good and to bear the burden of the suffering. For Augustine the "whole Christ" embraces Head and Body. Therefore, he can say to the faithful, "Let us rejoice, then, and give thanks that we are made not only Christians, but Christ."[5] The union of

Christ and humankind is a unity freely chosen out of love. Christ loves us, he wants to be one with us and in us, and he asks us to be one with him out of love.

"I have no hands but yours." With these words, Christ opens to us a space in which we live: the Church as the Body of Christ. This figure of the "*whole* Christ" as the Wounded Healer opens an ecumenical perspective. The love of Jesus is like a house in which we can live. Christ is the Head of the Body, the Communion of the Church. We are his limbs, his hands, his feet, and his shoulders.

The words of the crucified and risen Lord "I have no hands but yours" refer to a Christian way of life, experienced not only by the heads of churches, but also by the faithful, not only on the academic level but in the practice of everyday life as well. These words involve the people of God, particularly the worldwide communion of youth movements from different countries and different Christian traditions, all of them committed to the example of Christ, the Wounded Healer. Hands that labor and toil, hands that work and play, hands that pray and thank. Feet that step through rain and sun, and that walk on paths of peace. Shoulders that carry backpacks. This happens again and again in youth movements all over the world. So many young people work toward the same ideal, the same vocation, the same commitment: to give children space and freedom in a wide range of creative activities. Even if a society does not dare, or cannot believe it, all these good things happen because the risen Lord says, "I have no hands but yours." Christian spirituality concerns the lived spirituality of these young people who are engaged in love for Christ, who is still suffering or sick, locked up in prison on earth. Augustine was once young, and always he kept in contact with young people, before his conversion in school, after his conversion in the monastery, and throughout his episcopal ministry. His spirituality can encourage us to walk in communion of the whole Christ as pilgrims toward the heavenly Jerusalem.

THE CHURCH AS COMMUNION IN PILGRIMAGE

For Augustine, Christian life can be compared to a pilgrimage. His *Confessions* are a review of his conversion and inner pilgrimage toward God, a deep confession of his fragility and sinful existence. Augustine developed a theology of pilgrimage, not only with regard to his own life, but also with regard to the Church, the Body of Christ and the life of a Christian. Christian spirituality can be inspired by Augustine's spirituality of the communion of the Church in pilgrimage to the heavenly Jerusalem. The idea of Church as communion, as people of God, proposed and supported by the Second Vatican Council, has roots in the teaching of Saint Augustine.

Augustine developed a dynamic view of the Church as the Body of Christ, enlivened by the Holy Spirit, and of the Church as communion. The Church as communion participates in the unity of the Father, the Son, and the Holy Spirit. Augustine's view of the Church deals with the concept of unity in diversity, diversity in universality; the Church as sacramental and spiritual communion; the earthly and the heavenly Church, the Pilgrim Church, and the Church in its eschatological fulfillment.[6]

The Church as a Sacramental Communion

Common Baptism as Unity in Faith

Christian spirituality is a sacramental spirituality, based on our common baptism by which we are already through the one Spirit members of the one Body of Christ and live in a profound spiritual communion as unity in faith.

According to the Donatists, the validity of the sacraments depended on the holiness of the minister. Augustine responded, saying that the validity of baptism does not depend on the holiness of the minister, but on Christ. The purity of the minister is irrelevant because the purity and power of Christ is what makes baptism effective.

Augustine wants to emphasize the unique position of Christ in baptism. Baptism is the gift of Christ. "So long as we continue to be baptized, Jesus baptizes."[7] Augustine held that every baptism in the name of the Father and the Son and the Holy Spirit is valid. Everyone who has been baptized is baptized into the Church because it is the baptism of Christ and of the Church.

Augustine appeals to the analogy of a soldier. Soldiers normally were branded on the back of the right hand. This brand was meant to deter desertion, since it was extremely difficult to remove. The Catholic Church recognized in their baptism the authentic baptism of Christ. Augustine claimed that the Donatists were baptized validly, affirming that "just as soldiers who deserted were not re-branded, so those who received baptism outside the church were not to be rebaptized."[8] Augustine repeatedly emphasizes that those who received baptism even outside the Church were not to be rebaptized, referring to baptism as a spiritual birth. Augustine recognizes the validity of baptism administered outside the ecclesial community.

The first step to unity in Christ is unity in the faith of the Church and in the confession of faith, expressed in the baptismal (Apostle's) Creed. The confession of faith remains common to the Churches of both East and West and is a sign of recognition and communion among Christians. Christians have to be encouraged to rediscover the riches of their baptism and faith by gathering together for celebrations. In this way, they become closer to Jesus Christ and to one another.

Baptism is the sacrament of new birth, the sacrament of faith. Faith establishes a living, durable, and interpersonal relationship between the faithful and Christ. The Church is built on a communion of faith. Augustine encourages the faithful to advance in the faith of Christ, to believe in him, to come into communion with him. Christ dwells in human hearts through faith. Faith can grow step by step, day by day, from root to an amazing tree. Faith is not only a gift, but also a personal act of taking steps to Christ. Faith is a gift of God and an act of the heart with the desire to approach Christ. Faith is an incorporation with Christ. Faith cannot be separated from charity. The unity of the Church is the fruit of the communion both in faith and in love. Christ makes man sharer of his own life through his Spirit of love. To believe in Christ is to love him, to cherish him, to go to him, and to be embodied as his members.

Eucharist: Sacrament of Devotion, Sign of Unity, Bond of Charity

The Eucharist is the sacrament of the Church. The Eucharist assimilates us into Christ to give us his Spirit to share with us his love for the Father and for humanity. Commenting on John 6:51—"The bread I will give is my flesh, for the life of the world"—Augustine pronounces one of the most famous syntheses of the Eucharist: "O mystery of piety! O sign of unity! O bond of charity."[9] This expression has been used many times in the history of theology and is quoted by the Second Vatican Council.

Augustine affirms successively that the eucharistic food and drink are the body and blood of the Lord. Christ gives in his flesh and blood what he is. The eucharistic body of

Christ nourishes the mystical body, communicates life to his members. Augustine states that the Eucharist is the sacrament of unity, the bread of concord, and the bond of love. Augustine explains the unity of the body and blood of Christ. Many things are reduced to one thing. A unity is formed by many grains together. And another unity is effected by the clustering together of many grapes.[10] In the Eucharist, the Holy Spirit transforms and assimilates more intimately to Christ those who are already united with him. He nourishes the members of Christ, he integrates them more profoundly to his body, and he brings them closer to one another in a living solidarity through the unifying strength of love. The love of God, which has been poured forth in our hearts by the Holy Spirit, makes many souls one soul and many hearts one heart. Therefore, Augustine defines the Eucharist as the bond of charity.

The Church as a Spiritual Communion

Augustine also describes the Church as a spiritual communion, referring to the unifying activity of the Holy Spirit, who keeps the Church together. According to Augustine, the Holy Spirit is the principle of communion and unity. One of the central benefits of the Holy Spirit is the unifying activity of the Spirit. The Spirit, who unites the Father and the Son as the bond of love and peace, can unify with the same love so many hearts and the Body of Christ. Augustine's dynamic view of the Church deals with the concepts of unity and diversity of the Church. The unifying love, which is the Holy Spirit, assembles all the members of the Body and unites them with the Head, Christ. We are all one in Christ, Head and members are one Christ. We all live by the same life and we are unified by the same Holy Spirit.

Augustine developed a community spirituality as a spirituality of unity within diversity, a unity in concordance with the model of the Trinity, one God in three persons, existing in an intimate exchange of love. The Second Vatican Council took up this thought further and described the concept of *communio* as the most profound mystery of the Church, which is modeled as an icon of the Trinity.[11] The unity given by the Spirit is not a uniform monotony but rather a unity of great diversity.

Augustine's dynamic view of the Church deals with the concepts of unity and diversity of the Church. The universality and unity of the Church are animated by the unifying love of the Holy Spirit. The Church, the people of God, is founded on Christ and animated by the Holy Spirit, who is the principle of life of the Church. Augustine emphasized strongly the unity and universality of the Church against the separatist movement of the Donatists. Augustine extended the notion of the Church by referring to the righteous of the Old Testament, who are made righteous by the Spirit who poured forth love in their hearts, the "Church from Abel."[12] For Augustine, Pentecost was neither the absolute beginning of the activity of the Spirit nor of the Word of God. The Spirit as the Word of God transcends the temporal limits of the history of Christianity. Christ communicated himself as Divine Word and Wisdom, even before he came into the world. Even before Jesus' birth, there existed a people of God: Abraham, Isaac, Jacob, Moses, and the other patriarchs as well as the other prophets who foretold the coming of Christ. The prophets did not foretell future events without the Holy Spirit. There is thus already a Church from the beginning of humanity.

The Church as an Eschatological Communion

Augustine also describes the Church as an eschatological communion. He develops a dynamic vision of the Church. He distinguishes many meanings that are related yet distinct from one another: the terrestrial and the celestial Church, the Church in time and space, and the Church as city of God or kingdom of heaven; the Pilgrim Church and its eschatological fulfillment. The Church is on the way, *ad interim* between the Easter of the Lord and our Easter. Augustine insisted on the distinction between the Church in this time (*qualis nunc est*) and the Church at the end (*qualis tunc erit*). Augustine makes the distinction between the terrestrial with good and bad and the heavenly and pure Church at the end of her pilgrimage. Therefore, Augustine speaks about the Church as a *corpus permixtum*, a mixed Body with good and evil, whereas in eternity it will have only the good.

Augustine wanted to approach the Church in a realistic manner. In the Church there is both good and evil. The real danger does not come from outside the Church, from paganism or from Donatism, but from within. The Church is a church of people. As the human condition is a mixture of good and evil, this also is true in the Church. The mixture of good and evil is not only something external, beyond me, but also in myself. In the human heart, there is light and darkness. The mixture of good and evil is also present in us. Augustine invites Christians to withhold judgments and to not judge anything before the time when the Lord enlightens the darkness and reveals the thoughts of the heart. Hence, Augustine calls us to look into our own hearts.

Augustine was very realistic. He had firsthand experiences of the pain of a Church wounded by conflict. In open controversy with the Donatists, he wanted at all costs to promote unity, achieved in charity. For the Donatists, the Church is only comprised of saints. According to Augustine, the Church is a composite, a *corpus permixtum* embracing in its bosom both saints and sinners. The presence of good and evil in the Church is a reality, for the Church is composed of human beings. The mixture of good and evil is a characteristic of the Church in her earthly phase. Today the Church is on pilgrimage, in exile, roaming. The Church is still under construction. Augustine calls the Church a kingdom, but it is still under construction, it is still being prepared. This kingdom does not yet reign. The Church must extend, must be purified and sanctified, and must grow toward unity and peace.

Augustine invites the faithful to develop a conscience of pilgrimage, to run with him by believing, to believe that they are foreigners, pilgrims.[13] The Church is on the road, *ad interim*, between the Easter of the Lord and our Easter. The Church is on the road to the heavenly Easter. Augustine reminds the faithful that they are making a journey and that their life is an inn.[14] He reflects that on this journey, which is our lifetime, we must meditate upon nothing else except the fact that we shall not always be here. The Holy Spirit teaches us that we are in exile, he teaches us to sigh for our native land. The Church is the pilgrim people of God en route in the history of the world.

The pilgrimage of the Church is a long journey of groaning, of love and tears, of longing for the celestial homeland. Augustine calls the faithful to desire the heavenly homeland "where we live with good affection, without any want… where there is no hungering nor thirsting; where immortality is fullness, and truth our aliment."[15] With a rich language of images, Augustine evokes the eternal life, where people are to fear nothing, where they are to be untroubled, where they are not to die. It will be festivity, pure joy without end, eternity without blemish, serenity without a cloud. It will be happiness, joy, and peace. There will be full and perfect freedom. In God's house there is salvation and rest without end. Such an end will not have an end. Christ will fill us with himself. God will be all in all. We will see the naked light itself. Then we will find true pastures, where we who hunger and thirst after justice are to have our fill. There will not be any envy, because the unity of love will reign in all.

"We Are Sojourners"[16]

Augustine uses the words *pilgrim, pilgrimage, to make a pilgrimage* to make clear that our life in this world is a journey in exile toward God. We are sojourners, foreigners; we are taking a trip in a wasteland toward the center of our hearts. The true pilgrimage is the pilgrimage of the heart.

Augustine, as bishop of Hippo, knew very well the dangers of the sea, of waves and surf, both from his own experience and from contact with the seafaring people that he met in the port city. Therefore, the theme of the sea is very popular in the writings of Augustine. The sea, with its many dangers, the tumult of its storms, represents the century, the time of this world.[17]

The image of the disciples who cross the lake of Capernaum in the darkness and the storm is the symbol of the terrestrial pilgrimage of the Church through all the difficulties of a world in time and space. According to Augustine, we are all temples of God and every one of us is sailing a boat in his heart. Augustine describes the critical situation when he speaks of the darkness and of Jesus who had not yet come. In the darkness, errors, iniquity, and unbelief grow, and terror becomes frequent. This darkness refers to love grown cold and the increase of hatred among brothers. In many of his sermons Augustine uses the image of the raging waves to refer to the tribulations and the persecutions that Christians have to undergo, or of the storm to evoke the temptations incited by personal passions. "You have heard an insult, it is a high wind. You have got angry, it is a wave. So as the wind blows and the waves break, the boat is in peril, your heart is in peril, your heart is tossed about."[18]

Augustine emphasizes how, despite those winds, storms, and waves, a ship might overcome such troubles and proceed. No one can cross the sea of this world unless carried by the cross of Christ, the boat that carries the disciples, the Church. When the storm is raging, Augustine invites the faithful to remain in the boat and to remember Christ. "Don't let the waves overwhelm when your heart is upset by a temptation...don't let us despair. Let us wake up Christ, and so sail on in a calm sea, and reach our home country."[19] Augustine continues his comment by citing the story of Jesus walking on water. While treading on the waves, Jesus has all the swellings of the world under his feet—he presses upon all the heights of this age, he presses down all the ambitions of this age. Finally, the disciples take him on to the ship, recognizing him and rejoicing.

"Run with Me"[20]

Augustine did not like to travel, but due to his responsibilities he had to leave his diocese many times. Augustine participated in about ten councils at Carthage, about 155 miles away, which took eight to ten days of travel. He was invited to speak at Church gatherings about fifty times, traveling about the same distance. He was regularly invited to deliver homilies outside his own city. Augustine always walked or rode on a donkey, in poverty and humility.[21]

Augustine's thought on pilgrimage can be a source of encouragement on the way toward peace and harmony. Augustine invites us to walk together, to run by believing, by hoping, by desiring. When Augustine invites Christians to undertake a pilgrimage, he does not speak first about bodily footsteps, but about the footsteps of the heart, the pilgrimage of the heart, the pilgrimage of inner harmony. Augustine invites us to develop a spirituality of togetherness. During our pilgrimage, something happens inside. We undertake an inner journey, toward the heart of our churches and our communities, Christ. We are all members of his Body. He and we, the Head and the Body, the "whole Christ," animated by his Spirit. Day by day, we realize that we are on the way that we have to walk together, with Christ. Step by step, we realize that the journey itself makes us pilgrims for unity. We all undertake our pilgrimage. We cannot do this by ourselves. We are all vulnerable and we have all the same Teacher, who leads the way.

Augustine encourages us to develop together a "traveling heart," a "journey of the heart." Walking and running mean to make progress, to move on, to make progress in seeking the good, in good conduct. We must walk, we must make progress, we must grow, that our hearts may be able to hold those things that we cannot now hold. Walking entails living in the presence of the Lord. On our walk, we thirst together for justice and peace.

"Let Us Purify Our Hearts"[22]

The pilgrim's labyrinth of Chartres has the shape of a wheel. Human life can be compared with a wheel moving along the road, contaminated by dirt and mud. The history of the Church has known glorious days, but also dark times marked by discord and painful conflicts. The spirituality of Augustine shows us the way of conversion. Christian spirituality entails a journey on the road of purification, *purgatio*, asking the Lord that he might take away the dust and dirt from our path, that we might be freed from our baggage, with all its ballast of evil and darkness from the past, that he might cleanse our hearts.

In many of his writings and speeches, Pope Benedict XVI evokes the conversion of Saint Augustine as a spiritual pilgrimage through different phases or periods, as a journey that continued to the end of his life.

In his *Confessions*, Augustine described the development of his conversion, which was not a single act, but a journey through his whole life. This journey did not end when he received baptism the night before Easter 387, but also continued so that one can speak of different steps, three milestones in the whole process of conversion.[23]

The first step to his conversion was in his progressive nearing to Christianity. He received a Christian education from his mother Monica. As a passionate seeker of truth, he studied philosophy, which led him even closer to Christ. By reading the *Hortensius* of Cicero and through initiation into Neo-Platonism, he was strengthened in his search for wisdom.[24] However, only the Letters of Saint Paul fully revealed the truth to him.

One day in the garden of his home in Milan, he was torn between two minds. His good friend Alypius was with him. Then he heard the voice of a child from the neighboring house repeating several times, "Take up and read." Augustine was doubtful about whether it was a game of children singing such words or a sign from heaven. Augustine opened the Bible and found the text of Romans 13:13–14: "Let us live honorably as in the day, not in reveling and drunkenness, not in debauchery and licentiousness, not in quarreling and jealousy. Instead, put on the Lord Jesus Christ, and make no provision for the flesh, to gratify its desires."[25] Augustine realized that these words were a message to his heart: "No further would I read, nor did I need; for instantly, as the sentence ended—by a light, as it were, of security infused into my heart—all the gloom of doubt vanished away."[26] Augustine realized that only faith in the humble Christ could fulfill his long journey of seeking for truth.

After his baptism, Augustine established a monastery with a group of friends and dedicated his life to contemplation and study of the Bible. Three years later, he was ordained priest against his will, realizing fully how radically his life would change. This was the second step. He understood that only by living for others, and not simply for his private contemplation, could he really live with Christ and for Christ. Renouncing a life of meditation, Augustine learned to make the fruit of his intelligence available to others, to communicate his faith to simple people, and to translate the gospel into the language of everyday life. As he described in one of his sermons, he would be "reprimanding the undisciplined, comforting the faint-hearted, supporting the weak, refuting opponents...encouraging the negligent, soothing the quarrelsome, helping the needy, liberating the oppressed, expressing approval to the good, tolerating the wicked and loving all."[27]

Finally, Pope Benedict refers to a third conversion that brought Augustine to ask God for forgiveness every day of his life. Augustine had learned "the humility of recognizing that he himself and the entire pilgrim Church needed and continually need the merciful goodness of a God who forgives every day."[28] During an audience, Pope Benedict said, referring to Augustine, "We always need to be washed by Christ, who washes our feet, and be renewed by him. We need permanent conversion. Until the end we need this humility that recognizes that we are sinners journeying along, until the Lord gives us his hand definitively and introduces us into eternal life."[29]

Augustine's conversion is not the result of a philosophical reflection but of his imitation of the humble Christ.

"The Church Is Always in Need of Being Purified"[30]

Saint Augustine developed a realistic and humble view of the Church as *corpus permixtum*, a mixed Body, a Body of saints and sinners. The presence of good and evil in the Church is a reality, for the Church is composed of human beings. The mixture of good and evil is a character-istic of the Church in her earthly phase. The Church is under construction. She is in the process of becoming the perfect Body of Christ.

In this time of the earthly Church's pilgrimage to the eschatological heavenly Church, Augustine invites Christians to travel away from the false life, to cleanse the heart by faith, and to prepare by leading a holy life.[31] Augustine frequently uses the image of the exodus to refer to Christ who cleanses the Church by the bath of water in the Word in baptism. As the Israelites passed through the Red Sea, while the Egyptians perished in that sea, so the candidates would pass through the Red Sea of baptism. The Church has still to seek unity and peace. The life of the Church is not only a wait for the end of time. We are also called to build the Church now so that we make progress in peace and unity and that we may belong to the Communion of Saints. Augustine invites the faithful to bow their heads in humility before the humble Christ, to accept the terrestrial Church as a community with good and bad, giving up pride, wearing the robes of humility and charity. Conversion, a change of heart and mind, is necessary for the purification of our memories. Conversion also supposes a *kenosis*, an emptying of oneself. *Kenosis* opens the way to recognition of faults and sins, the achievement of a sincere repentance and gestures of pardon. This *kenotic* way requires humility.

Augustine invited the faithful to travel as pilgrims on the road to the heavenly Jerusalem, bearing each other's bur-dens and pain through a process of reconciliation and heal-ing of wounds, growing in faith, hope, and love. Referring to the scandal of the broken Christ and of divided Christianity, we can express the hope that all Christians might walk together on the road of charity through humility, prayer and penitence, to heal the wounds of the blessed and broken Body of Christ.

"The Singers of the New Song"[32]

In his comment on the new commandment of the Lord, Augustine develops the theme of "the singers of the new song." Augustine connects the new song with the new commandment of Jesus, that we should love one another, as he also has loved us. Augustine comments that this commandment is very old because it can be already found in Leviticus 19:18, but it is also new because this commandment transforms us into a new being and because it is a call to love as Christ has loved us. "This is the love that renews us, making us new men, heirs of the New Testament, singers of the new song. It was this love, brethren beloved, that renewed also those of olden time, who were then the righteous, the patriarchs and prophets."[33]

Singing together can be very valuable in deepening spiritual ecumenism. At the time of Augustine, an important development had taken place regarding singing in church. Ambrose introduced the Eastern tradition of allowing the faithful to sing the psalm verses. Augustine became a great promoter of this in North Africa. Augustine loved light, harmony, and singing. He wept when listening to the sacred hymns of Ambrose at the time of his conversion. At the same time, he warned of the danger that people would be more fascinated by the beautiful voice of a singer than by the content of the song. Singing is valuable because it is first and foremost a praise of God. The great riches of the poor Body of Christ on earth are expressed in song. In his description of singing, Augustine emphasizes the transition from voice to heart, from the outside to the inner. "The one who sings praise, not only praises, but also praises joyfully; the one who sings praise, not only sings, but also loves Him for whom he sings."[34]

Singing together songs of longing strengthens the prayerful heart. When we are working, or when we are resting, these songs continue in the heart. Augustine invites Christians to walk in Christ, to chant the song of a longing heart. "For he who truly longs, thus sings within his soul, though his tongue be silent: he who does not, however he may resound in human ears, is voiceless to God."[35]

Augustine invites his audience to sing as pilgrims, longing for heavenly happiness. Prayerful longing broadens and expands the heart. Therefore, we sing the Alleluia for fifty days after Easter; we sing love songs of the heavenly fatherland as a foretaste of eternal happiness. Augustine speaks about walking in the Way and singing in this Way a new song. "Sing the love-songs of your fatherland, let no one sing old ones. New Way, new wayfarer, new song."[36] He who sings in a part, sings an old song: he is divided. He, who sings in the Spirit, sings a new song.

Augustine puts the emphasis on the harmony between singing and love, between singing and the righteous life. He invites the faithful to sing en route, not to delight their leisure, but to ease their toil. "Keep on walking" means to go onward always…in goodness, onward in the right faith, onward in good habits and behavior. Augustine describes a song as a thing of joy, as a thing of love. If someone has learned to love the new life, he has learned to sing a new song, and the new song reminds us of our new life. The new man, the new song, the new covenant, all belong to the one kingdom of God, and so the new man will sing a new song and will belong to the new covenant.

Augustine expresses the importance of singing not just with the mouth, but also with the heart and deeds. He invites the faithful to make sure that their life does not contradict their words, to sing with their voices, their hearts, their lips, and their lives. If someone desires to praise the Lord, then he must live what he expresses. "Live good lives, and you yourselves will be his praise."[37]

CHAPTER 5

Ecclesial Charity

Love is at the center in the preaching and the spirituality of Augustine. Augustine was aware that he never could speak enough of love. Love is the most profound and mysterious element in the human person. The purpose of Augustine's preaching is to arouse enthusiasm for the true love of God and neighbor. Therefore, Augustine has been called the doctor of charity.

TRINITARIAN LOVE

The pilgrim's labyrinth in Chartres includes the motif of the circle, which refers to God's immutable and incomprehensible love. God is unconditional love and his love is eternal, without beginning and without end.

For Augustine, the unity of the Church is grounded in the trinitarian love among Father, Son, and Holy Spirit. The trinitarian love among the Father, the Son, and the Holy Spirit is the basis or foundation for Christian and Church unity. God is the beginning and the source of every love. Love is the gift of divine life to humankind, the greatest gift of all his benefits. The love of the Trinity is prior, before the foundation of the world. God has loved us first. The Father loved us before we existed, in an incomprehensible way.[1]

The most important manifestation of the love of the Father is the sending of his Son. In his mercy, God sent his only Son to share our death and to lead us to his immortality. He suffered and died to purify us from sin. At the cross, Jesus cured our wounds, which he endured as his own. He healed us of eternal death when he deigned to die a temporal death. Through his love, Christ has identified himself with us that we may become a whole Body, Christ, the Head, and we the members.[2] Through his immense grace we should be bound together by mutual love.[3]

Because God has loved us first, he sent not only the incarnate Son but also the Holy Spirit, the source, the fountain of love. The Spirit poured forth love in our hearts. Love is the greatest benefit of the Holy Spirit in us. Love comes to us through the mercy of God, through the Holy Spirit. According to Augustine, we have to love with the love that has been poured forth in our hearts by the Holy Spirit. Divine love must inspire our human love. Therefore, Augustine refers to the new commandment that Christ has given to us: that we love one another as Christ also has loved us. This love renews us that we may be new men, singers of a new song. We can love only through the Holy Spirit. The Holy Spirit in us inspires us to the love of God and the love of our neighbor. Unity is a gift of the Holy Trinity, a gift of the love of God. The unity of the Church is based upon the unity of the Holy Trinity. God gives himself and communicates himself as Father and Son and as both in the Holy Spirit. The Holy Spirit who is the bond of charity of the Father and the Son is the soul of the Body of Christ.

By contemplating the Trinity, we are called to overcome divisions, to transform discord into concord, to become "of one heart and soul." Imitating the Trinity is a call to imitate its example of unity in diversity. The Church is communion and communion is the fruit and demonstration that springs from the Holy Trinity to make us *of one heart and one soul.*

Augustine repeats that unity is the fruit of love. Love draws human beings beyond the boundaries of ego. In fact, every virtue—such as temperance, fortitude, justice, prudence—is a form of love. Even the simple virtues of daily life are forms of love. Nobody can be peaceful, benevolent, faithful, mild, or honest, without love. Love is the heart of Christian life.

Love brings together and creates unity. Love renews the nations, gathers a new people, the Body of the new Spouse, the Bride of the Son of God. Through love, multiplicity is gathered in unity. Augustine calls to unity, to be one, to be one person.[4] Contemplating the unifying force of love, Augustine describes love as the bond that keeps the Church united. Ecclesial unity is especially a gift of love because love unifies not only the ideas but also the wills of men. Charity unites the members to the Church, the Body of Christ. Where there is charity, there is unity and vice versa. We have charity if we embrace unity. The Holy Spirit is the source of charity and charity is the source of unity. Charity is like unity indivisible.

According to Augustine unity is not an unrealistic sentimentalism but a starting point for concrete ecclesial apostolic action. Augustine emphasizes repeatedly that unity is the fruit of charity through humility and conversion. Augustine discovered the mercy to contemplate the "beauty of the Holy Trinity" through activities such as prayer, study, and charity. These three activities express the trinitarian dimension of conversion. Praying is the attitude of humility, because through this act man is able to recognize that everything is a gift of the Father. Study means listening to the voice of wisdom as it is revealed in Christ. Loving is putting one's life under the guidance of love, the Holy Spirit.

"LOVE WITH ME"⁵

Regularly using the expression "love with me, run with me by believing," Augustine invited the faithful to love God and their neighbor on their pilgrimage to the heavenly homeland. In our pilgrimage, we are not alone, because Christ is with us, our Way, and our Light. Therefore, our pilgrimage of love is a way in joy and light because we are sure that we are on the road with him and that we receive his mercy, which is our joy. If we love God, we cannot despise his command to love our neighbor.

Augustine emphasizes the unity and the harmony of love for God and neighbor.⁶ The basis of the inseparability of the two commandments is the idea of the "whole Christ," where Christ identifies himself with the members of his Body through love. The use of Matthew 25:31–46—"Just as you did it to one of the least of these who are members of my family, you did it to me"—plays a role in Augustine's vision of the relationship between love for neighbor and love for God. The Head of Christ and the members of the Body cannot be separated. Christ still suffers on earth in his members. Christ identifies himself with the least of these. One cannot love one's neighbor authentically without loving God. Continuing on this thought, Augustine says that the love of God can be tested in everyday practice. The love of neighbor can easily be observed and checked. Love of God begins with the love of neighbor. The love of neighbor becomes concrete in the respect for everyone's individuality, in promoting the welfare of others, in seeking the good for others. The love of God for us is visible and palpable in our love for one another. Our love for one another is a sign of God in this world.

Augustine keeps the love of God and love of neighbor together. Without love for man, our love of God is not real.

Without love of God, our love for man is powerless. Love of God touches people. Love for others shows that the love of God is real. First, there is the fact that God loves us, that there is a power of divine love in this world. Second, Augustine, who was deeply impressed by the experience of human love and friendship, gradually came to believe that the love of God for man and love between people is really the same love. Therefore, Augustine inverts the words *God is love* to *love is God*. Augustine emphasized that to love Christ entails extending our charity throughout the world, for the members of Christ are spread the world over. Evoking the universal dimension of the "whole Christ," Augustine developed a spirituality of togetherness through ecclesial charity.

A Spirituality of Togetherness through Ecclesial Charity

Augustine wanted to strengthen the desire for the true love of God and neighbor. The Head of the Body of Christ cannot be separated from the members of the Body. Augustine highlights that those who love the members also love the Head of the Body of Christ. The fraternal love that unites Christians in the Body of Christ constitutes the first circle of the love of neighbor. Augustine sets further steps in his sermons when he calls the faithful to love their enemies, as well as the alienated, and the poor.

Many times Augustine implores his hearers to the love of their enemies, which is considered the perfect love. Even if an enemy hates us, we must pray for him. For Augustine it is very clear that by so doing, we also advance in love and this love forms and restores the image of God in us. When a Christian prays for an enemy, he imitates the Divine Master and he resembles him, as Saint Paul, Saint Stephen, and so many martyrs of Christ have already done.

The call to "love with me" is linked with titles Augustine gives to those who come to listen to him—"brothers, my brethren, dearly beloved"—to express his affection, his attachment, and his loyalty. Especially in the time of the controversies with the Donatists, he calls the faithful "beloved," to explain to them that they belong to the Church spread throughout the world and that the Church is the place of unity, peace, and charity. Many times, he addresses even the Donatists with a fraternal and fatherly greeting. Saint Augustine tries to involve all Christians in unity with Christ. When addressing Catholics, Augustine invites them not to engage in discussions and polemics with the separated brethren, but rather to demonstrate deep love for them. Augustine invites them to pray for the separated, to preach, and to love. In this way, they will see the deep pain of separation. Augustine expresses these sentiments because he also suffers great sorrow over the controversy. Even if he spoke and lamented all day, even if his tears flowed like a fountain, even if he changed into tears, it would not be enough. Augustine invites the faithful to approach the Donatists with prayer, with invitation, with fasting.

For Augustine, the poor are the most precious group in the Church, because they represent the weak and needy Christ.[7] Augustine entreats the faithful to feed the hungry Christ, to give water to the thirsty Christ, to clothe the naked Christ, to visit the sick Christ, and to welcome the foreigner-Christ.[8] The Church has to develop a special care for the poor and the oppressed. In this context, Augustine evokes the Gospel where Mary anointed Jesus' feet with perfume and wiped them with her hair. Augustine explains that for the faithful the luxury of perfume and hair seem to be a superfluity, but for the Lord's feet they may be a necessity, because perhaps on earth the Lord's feet are in need.

The poor are constantly present in Augustine's sermons and his pastoral activity. As a real ambassador of the poor, Augustine expressed his desire to become one with them: "making myself a beggar with the beggars."[9] In his sermons Augustine often described his pastoral commitment to the poor: "To rebuke those who stir up strife, to comfort those of little courage, to take part of the weak, to refute opponents, to be on guard against traps, to teach the ignorant…to help the poor to liberate the oppressed, to encourage the good, to suffer the evil, and to love all."[10]

Augustine considered care of the poor more important than liturgical ornaments. He was convinced of the need to practice an ecclesial charity for the poor and not to ignore their empty stomachs. When a rich ship owner wanted to give his ships to Augustine, he answered, "It is not the task of a bishop to save up gold and to push away the hand of the beggar."[11] Through a concrete application of his thought on the "whole Christ," Augustine emphasized that Christ is still needy, suffering, and poor. We are touching Christ when we help the poor. In the face of the poor, we recognize the face of the Lord. Augustine devoted himself constantly to an ecclesial charity for Christ who is still lying on the street, Christ who still hungers and thirsts, Christ who is still cold.

Augustine's spirituality of a tangible ecclesial charity is a call to develop a spirituality of togetherness by taking care of the poor for the "needy Christ." Christian spirituality is a matter of charity that rises from the fervent prayer for the reunification of the Christian family. Reflecting on God's power, which has been revealed and incarnated in Jesus Christ as the self-emptying, self-giving power of love, the Church has to express the need for ecclesial charity in order to empower the helpless and the poor.

A Spirituality of Hospitality and Friendship

Augustine developed a spirituality of hospitality. The Church is a place "wherein the wounded are healed just like the travelers' inn in the parable of the Good Samaritan."[12] Augustine refers to the Good Samaritan to encourage the faithful to gain an understanding of universal love. According to Augustine, the parable reveals the gratuitous love of Christ for mankind.[13] The word *Samaritan* means "guardian" and refers to our Savior Jesus Christ. The Samaritan poured the oil of consolation, the wine of exhortation; he healed the wounds of the traveler and brought him to an inn. He entrusted him to the innkeeper, whom Augustine also sees as an ambassador for Christ. The Samaritan left two coins to pay for the care of the traveler. Augustine interprets these two coins as the two precepts on which the whole Law and the Prophets are based. The inn is the Church in which the travelers can enjoy hospitality, in which the wounded are healed.

As strangers, we are guests in this world, pilgrims going to the heavenly homeland. This world is a way station, an inn. Therefore, Augustine presented himself as a good host, and he encouraged others to practice hospitality. Christ too is a pilgrim, a stranger in this world. Because he became man, we can welcome him in this world and in this way prepare a place for him in this world, that he also will prepare a place for us in heaven. Many times Augustine affirms in his sermons that whoever receives the poor foreigner, receives Christ. Since Christ will appear as a stranger or guest, the practice of hospitality for him is the occasion to acquire a deeper knowledge of Christ. Augustine links the practice of hospitality with the "Christ-experience." Christ is the "whole Christ," the Head and the Body. There is no point in praising oneself for doing a good act, because through this, God offers us the opportunity to receive his blessing and mercy. By receiving a stranger in hospitality, we get the chance to do something good for others.

Augustine invited the faithful to bear each other's burdens along the way. Referring to the deer that cross a stream, looking for a grassy meadow on an island, walking in a row sequentially, carrying for each other their heavy antlers, Augustine encourages his listeners not only to carry one another's burdens, but also to be a beast of burden for the Lord.

Not only hospitality but also friendship can play an important role in human relationships. Augustine was the first Christian to elaborate a theory of Christian friendship. Starting from the classical concept of friendship as understood by Cicero, Augustine developed a concept of friendship as grace, a bond effected by the Holy Spirit.[14] We need to distinguish two periods in Augustine's teaching on friendship, namely the periods before and after the *Confessions*. In the first period, Augustine considered human sympathy the source of friendship, while in the second period he saw the bond of friendship as the gift of the Holy Spirit through grace. In fact, after the *Confessions*, Augustine spoke more about charity than friendship, but his love for friendship never disappeared. In his *Confessions* Augustine wrote that he could not make himself happy without friends. Augustine had very many friends. It is known how much he owed to his most trusted friend, Alypius.

Augustine saw true friendship as a grace, a gift of God, a bond of charity poured out in our hearts by the Spirit. True friendship has a perspective on eternity and is oriented toward God. Friendship can be considered as a pilgrimage in which friends orient their human familiarity toward the perfection of God. Friendship creates a unity with and in God. In his sermons, Augustine expressed the hope that we may be able to be the friends of the Lord and that we may be associated with his friendship. Our human friendship acquires a kind of permanency in Christ. God is the ultimate basis of loyal and steadfast friendship.

Bearing Witness to the Risen Lord

Martyrdom has a central place in Augustine's pastoral theology because Augustine linked martyrdom with patience and unity. Augustine puts the emphasis on the bond between Christ and the martyrs.[15] Christ is the Head Martyr himself, the martyrs are his members. Through their witness, they risk persecution and suffering. Christ is still suffering; the Church still suffers through the suffering of the martyrs. Martyrs bear witness; they confess the truth and die for it and for the name of Christ.

Augustine reacted against the idea of voluntary martyrdom promoted by the Donatists. Violent, armed groups within the Donatists, the *circumcelliones*, wreaked havoc, especially in rural areas. The *circumcelliones* were fanatical bands of vagrants who went out looting and attacking. Their conduct was motivated by nationalistic, social, and political factors. Poverty and poor social conditions were the reasons for their rebellion. Their opposition to the Roman state drove them to the Donatists, who opposed the Catholic Church that was under the protection of the Roman state. In their struggle against the emperor, the *circumcelliones* stole goods from the Catholic Church and tortured and executed Catholic priests. They even engaged in suicide missions as a form of martyrdom. The Donatists maintained good relations with the *circumcelliones* although they also distanced themselves from them. Violence against Catholics was a pious act, especially against former Donatists who converted to Catholicism or against Catholics who opposed them. Augustine was such an enemy. He once avoided an ambush because he took the wrong road.

Augustine emphasized repeatedly that these suicide martyrs follow the wrong examples and that they also lack patience. Augustine accused Donatist suicide martyrs of demonstrating their impatience by preferring to end their lives. Augustine considered martyrdom an imitation of the patience of Christ during his passion and as a witness of love for Christ. Patience is a Christian virtue necessary for avoiding suicide martyrdom and for overcoming pride. Christ gave the capacity of patience to his Church, to allow the martyrs to endure the ills and hardships inflicted on them.

Augustine not only made the link between martyrdom and patience, but also between martyrdom and unity. The Donatist movement was one of separation, while true martyrdom required union with the Church. True martyrs teach unity, while the Donatist martyrs are false martyrs because they teach divisiveness. Through their death, true martyrs give witness of the charity that unites the members of the Church. Augustine puts the emphasis on the link between the charity of the martyrs and unity with the Church. The origin of martyrdom is love. Real martyrdom is love, which is self-abnegation and creates a unity in the Body of Christ. True martyrs give witness of the charity that unites the members of the Church through their patience and humility.

According to Augustine, it is the Spirit of God, the Spirit of love, who inspires the verbal witness of the martyrs. The Spirit not only provides this verbal testimony but also the witness in deed that testifies to the Christian's eternal life. In *Tractate* 92 Augustine says that the Spirit empowered the disciples to bear witness to the risen Lord. Referring to the Spirit-filled Peter, Augustine sees the Spirit as an agent of renewal, who kindles frigid hearts, opens locked lips, and transforms diffidence to confidence, fear of speaking the truth into confession of the risen Lord.[16]

In his *Confessions* Augustine described the Holy Spirit as "the gravity of love, the upward pull which resists the downward gravity and brings everything to fulfillment in God."[17] The Spirit is not an immanent force in the human person, but the life given and empowered by God. The *Spiritus Creator* is at work in the whole reality of creation. Therefore, a spirituality of the Holy Spirit has to start from a universal perspective.

A Vision of Peace

Augustine delivers many reflections on peace. The word *pax* appears about 2,500 times in Augustine's writings. Augustine's Cathedral in Hippo was called the Basilica of Peace. Augustine had become a strong supporter and promoter of peace, often preaching about peace.

To have peace there must be internal and external peace or harmony. Internal peace concerns the balance between body and soul and good health. One can only find complete peace within oneself when one is free from temptation, hunger, thirst, illness, and tiredness. In fact, there will be the enduring battle to retain that peace. External peace refers to the relationship with other human beings, which Augustine calls *concordia*, oneness of heart.

Augustine makes the distinction between earthly peace and peace in the heavenly city. Augustine comments on the words of Jesus in John 14:27: "Peace I leave with you; my peace I give you." Jesus leaves peace with us in this age, but this peace has its own limits and is partial because the human being will always be divided in his inner self, between his good will and his impulses. Sin brought discord, hatred, and misunderstanding among men. The peace of which Jesus speaks is already possible, so that even here and now we may love one another. This peace is earthly, fragile, and incomplete because there is no true oneness of heart: "There can be no true peace where there is no real harmony, because their hearts are at variance."[18]

The peace of heaven will be true and complete peace, free of all strife. Augustine refers to the words of Jesus: "My peace I give you." Jesus leaves his peace with us. There we will be without an enemy. There we shall never be able to disagree. There we will have the face-to-face vision of God. This peace will be complete in a union of hearts, a *concordia* between creature and Creator. This heavenly peace evokes the vision of the peace of the Sabbath, which has no evening, the eternal peace where we shall rest and see, see and love, love and praise.

Augustine calls the faithful to peace, internal and external, to concord. Although they cannot be said to be without quarrel, they are commanded to build peace, the true and perfect peace. Augustine invites the faithful to return to themselves, to look into their own hearts and to cry out, and from their inner conflict to shout to God, hoping that he may bring inner peace. Finally, we will have peace in Christ who is our true Peace, the very goal in which our being Christian is entirely involved. After Pentecost the Apostles, who had fled from city to city, did not flee from Christ. They were refugees, but not from Christ; rather, he was their refuge, so they might have peace in him.[19]

According to Augustine, peace entails togetherness, communion, *concordia*, oneness of heart. In the beginning of his *Rule* Augustine refers to the religious character of a common taste of peace attained by dwelling together in unity and being of one mind and one heart in God, remembering that they have come together for this goal. At the end of the *Rule* Augustine calls the monks lovers of beauty, who in their affection for one another emanate the sweet odor of Christ as an aroma of peace.

In his *Sermons on the Gospel of Saint John* Augustine develops the theme of the kiss of peace that unifies the circumcised and the uncircumcised in the one faith of Christ, listening together to the voice of the Cornerstone. Augustine also describes the kiss of the dove, which symbolizes the Holy Spirit. The kiss of the dove arouses and creates peace, simplicity, goodness, patience, hope, sign of true love and unity. The kiss of the dove has to be distinguished from the kiss of the ravens. In ravens, there is a false peace. They kiss but they lacerate, they feed on death.

In *Tractate* 1 Augustine expresses the hope that there will be peace in the Church, referring to Psalm 71(72):3: "Let the mountains receive peace for your people, and the hills justice" (Vulgate/Douay-Rheims). Augustine expresses the greeting of peace of the mountains to the Church: peace be with you. This reference at the beginning of his sermons shows the deep concern of Augustine for true peace and real unity in the Church. Augustine can help us to walk together as pilgrims in this life to the New Jerusalem, the city of peace, the very goal of our human existence. We need a spirituality of communion, not one of individualism or solitude, but a spirituality of solidarity and peace. If we long for peace, we have to build it through our human efforts, becoming real messengers of peace through our words and our acts. Above all peace is the Easter gift of the risen Lord. "Peace He leaves with us, that here also we may love one another."[20]

TOWARD A SPIRITUALITY OF MINISTRY

A Spirituality of Ministry, Rooted in the Love and the Humility of Christ

Augustine developed a spirituality of ministry, rooted in the love and the humility of Christ, the Good Shepherd. This spirituality brings us to a common source of inspiration on our journey toward Christian unity. His spirituality can be a guide and offers some basic attitudes for all those who exercise a ministry in the Church.[21]

A first anchor point is Augustine's constant reference to Christ, the Good Shepherd, when he speaks about ministry. Augustine was aware of being only a minister, a servant of Christ, a minister of the inner Master. In exercising ministry, Christ must be at the center. Christ is the fountain and the strength of our ministry. The real apostolate is undertaken in the service of the saving act of Christ. Service to Christ is at the same time service to the people entrusted by Christ. Many times, Augustine preached on the danger of pride and the desire to dominate, seeking one's own interests, instead of the interests of Christ.

Augustine warned about the risk of considering the flock of the faithful as the personal property of the bishop. Each pastor has to remember that the sheep are Christ's and not his. He has to seek the glory of Christ and not his own glory, the kingdom of Christ and not his own kingdom. In fact, the community of the Church belongs to Christ. Referring to chapter 10 of the Gospel of John, Augustine affirms that there is only one Shepherd, Christ. Apostles, bishops, the faithful are members of the one Shepherd. Sometimes Augustine referred to some ministers, who seek their own interests, pursuing temporal advantages, aspiring for gain, coveting honors from men. For Augustine, it was clear, "He who loves God does not love money much."[22]

Augustine's spirituality seems still to be very fresh and relevant because he insisted on the necessity of integrity, a harmony between words and deeds. A minister is called to give the example of a good life. For Augustine it is evident that every pastor is called not only to preach the Gospel but also to live it, giving a good example to the faithful. The only way to live the ministry is through love, imitating the example of Christ who came to heal humanity from pride and to lead it to humility.

The ministry of service through humility and love is a second anchor point. Augustine saw his office as a *sarcina*, a burden, or the pack that a soldier carries on his back. The vocation of the Church is to serve. The Church participates in the same mission of Christ, to be servant of love. Augustine called himself "a servant of Christ, a servant of his servants."[23] The pastor is a fellow disciple, a fellow servant (*condiscipulus, conservus*). We are all fellow disciples of the one Lord and the one Shepherd. Augustine's spirituality of ministry is based upon togetherness in the discipleship of the Lord.

Augustine not only expressed a deep bond of discipleship with the Lord, but he emphasized a togetherness of discipleship among all Christians through and in the Lord, who is the Head of the Body, which is the Church. The pastor is not in the first place a man of authority but one of the faithful. The pastor is a disciple and a Christian with the other Christians. For Augustine there is a mutual exchange between the pastor and the faithful. It is not only so that the bishop is faithful with the faithful, the minister shares in being Christian, but conversely, the faithful share in the serving ministry of the bishop. Augustine calls everyone, clerics and faithful alike, to serve the Lord, to obey the will of the Lord, acting out of love in humility, loving justice. With the help of his thought on the "whole Christ," Augustine expressed this brotherhood of all Christians frequently in his sermons. In one of his sermons, Augustine evoked this spirituality of togetherness in a wonderful way: "What I am for you terrifies me; what I am with you consoles me. For you I am a bishop; but with you I am a Christian. The former is a duty; the latter a grace. The former is a danger; the latter, salvation."[24]

Augustine outlined the road to develop a spirituality of Christian *diaconia* through humility. Ministry in the Church is not a matter of applause or success, or triumphalism, but of humility and self-emptying love. Humility is an essential quality of the journey of the heart to Christian unity. In his humility, Christ gathered his flock as the Good Shepherd, the Universal Pastor. Not only the bishops and priests, but every Christian is called to be a servant of the humble Christ, who washed the feet of his disciples. Every Christian must become an apostle of the Word and an example of a good life in humility through love.

Augustine repeated that without love, ministry risks becoming an exercise of power. The love for Christ is the foundation and presupposition of every pastoral ministry.

For Augustine the first mission of the Church is to invite, to call. The Church should be inviting, both in its inner dynamics of love and in its internal structures.[25] The Church invites only; with confidence, she entrusts judgment and condemnation to God. The mission of the Church is to invite through the servitude of love, without self-interest and corruption. We are not judges, but inviters, ministers.[26] The Church has to present herself as vulnerable, not primarily as an authoritarian institution but as a communion of faithful united with each other through baptism in the Lord. Love is the main pillar of faith and Church. "The Church is incomprehensible outside the love of God for us."[27] Yet the exterior is important for Augustine, although in fact, the interior and the exterior are inseparable. In this context, Augustine describes the Church as "Mother." It is the task of the Church to give birth to new children of God and to nourish them. The Church has to follow the example of Christ, who adapted himself as milk for little children and solid food for the advanced. Augustine describes God and the Church as the parents who brought us into life. We have to love these parents: Father God and Mother Church.[28] We have to love them both; whoever offends his mother, offends his father. Augustine makes the distinction between our first birth, which is from male and female, and our second birth, which is from God and the Church. The Church has to be merciful and charitable as a mother. The Church teaches us how to love God and neighbor. Here the notion of Church is broader than hierarchy, because all the faithful have to take part in the motherly task of the Church.[29]

The third anchor point is the ministry of unity. Augustine preached in his sermons about promoting the unity of the Church, which is a fruit of charity. The good pastor evokes the voice of the one Universal Pastor. Augustine believed that one of the main tasks of the Church is to promote unity. The bishop is called to imitate Christ, in humility and love. While pride causes separation, charity creates unity.

Augustine used the symbol of the tunic of Christ, woven from the top, to indicate the unity of the Church, which is held together by the bond of love.[30] It symbolizes the unity that comes from on high, from heaven. Through this sign, Jesus represented the unity of the Church. The coat woven from the top signifies charity and unity. Even the persecutors of Christ did not rend his garment. The tunic of Christ cannot be divided, charity cannot be divided. Christians, who divided the Church, rent the unity that is the tunic of charity.[31] One can divide the outer, visible, or human elements of the Church, but not its deeper unity, which is identified with the Holy Spirit. The pastors are called to live together with the faithful, united by one spirit in the one Body of Christ. Augustine himself promoted Christian unity through his writings and preaching. We are all one in Christ, who is the Head while we are his Body. With the help of the doctrine of the "whole Christ,"

Augustine prefigured the concept of Christian unity. Though we are many, the Holy Spirit, who dwells in us, unifies us. Augustine emphasized that the coming of the Holy Spirit can be recognized by the love of unity: "Know that you have the Holy Spirit when you allow your heart to adhere to unity through sincere charity."[32]

For Augustine the minister is a man of unity who listens to the Lord and acts. This responsibility requires a large dose of patience and wisdom. Therefore, the minister must pray for the gift of spiritual fatherhood. Imitating the example of Christ, the minister calls the faithful to unity, inviting them in respect and humility. The Church has to make judgments, but the important thing is that its judgments must be Christ-like. They must be directed to salvation, not condemnation.

Steps toward a "Primacy of Love"

In his preaching on John 21, Augustine meditates on themes such as the name Peter; the threefold request of Jesus, "Feed my sheep;" and the service of Jesus as a *ministry of love*. The Church is founded on Christ and received from him the keys to the kingdom of heaven in the person of Peter. Peter represents the whole Church, in whose name he received the power of binding and loosing sins. Augustine comments on the word of Jesus that expresses the pastoral commission with which Peter is charged, "Feed my sheep." The threefold question of Jesus and the threefold answer of Peter are at the basis of every ministry. Because Peter is able to love Christ, he is worthy to feed the flock of Christ. The triple confession refers to the threefold denial. The reply of Christ to Peter's threefold profession indicates the core of the ministry to feed the sheep of the Lord. Augustine repeats that it is a risk for the minister to consider the faithful as his own property. It is the duty of love to feed the flock of the

Lord and not his own flock. "Those who have this purpose in feeding the flock of Christ, that they may have them as their own, and not as Christ's, are convicted of loving themselves, and not Christ."[33] Augustine warns those who love only themselves: lovers of money, pride, blasphemy, arrogance, people without affection, without kindness. Christ said, "Feed my sheep." With these words, Augustine reflects that Christ invites us to feed his sheep, not ourselves, not to seek our own glory, but his glory in us, not our own lordship, but his lordship, to seek those things that are his, not those things that are from us. "Therefore, let us not love ourselves but him."[34] This humble service enriches the Church with noble and generous men who are called to exercise the ministry in the name of Christ.

In his comments on John 21, Augustine describes the service of Christ as a *officium amoris*, a service of love. Augustine felt the burden of his episcopate as a real service, but he also emphasized the root of this ministry of service, the root of love. Augustine considered his episcopate as a charge to be accepted as a manifestation of love for Christ.[35] It is the duty of love to feed the flock of the Lord.

"RETURN TO YOUR HEART":[36] THE CALL TO INTEGRITY

In the center of the pilgrim's labyrinth in Chartres is a rose. The rose is the symbol of spiritual enlightenment, has six petals, and refers to Mary, the Mother of Christ. Mary is a direct reference to the center of the labyrinth, Jesus Christ. For Augustine, Mary is above all a woman of faith. Mary invites the faithful to orient themselves to the Lord, and to undertake the pilgrimage to the heavenly Jerusalem, with a good portion of faith, a backpack full of hope, and with the dress of love.

"Return to Your Heart":[37] A Spirituality of Interiority

Augustine not only calls Christians to unity *ad extra* (with the Donatists) but also to unity *ad intra*, to integrity inside the Church. This road to integrity passes through interiority and presumes a process of purification, *purificatio*. Christian unity is an *ad intra* movement, and calls the faithful to conversion, moral integrity, and spiritual renewal in charity. Christians can witness to unity in diversity by building a peaceful community that is not torn apart by polemics and polarization. The charismatic dimension of the Church is realized above all in the change of heart and the sanctification of personal life. The stained glass windows of churches present saints, and when the sunlight shines through the windows, the light comes through them— saints are transparent, they accept God's light, which is shining in their lives and illuminating even the darkest side of the heart. Christian spirituality entails undertaking this pilgrimage of the heart, praying together for transparency, the *illuminatio*, the Divine Light of God's immense love in our lives and our hearts. The center of the pilgrim's labyrinth is an open space where six round petal-shapes are related to harmony and balance. Walking on the road of pilgrimage is walking through purification, illumination toward integration and harmony: *unio*.

Commenting on a verse of Isaiah (46:8), Augustine invites the faithful to return to the heart: "Return to the heart! Return! Where? To the Lord....You are wandering outside, an exile from yourself....Christ dwells in the inner self; in the inner self you will be renewed in the image of God."[38] Augustine emphasizes that first we have to return to the heart.

The interiority is a central theme in the spirituality of Augustine. According to Augustine the road into interiority is divided in three moments: "Do not go away from yourselves," "Return to yourself," "Transcend yourself."

Do not go away from yourselves. Augustine invites the faithful not to go away from themselves. This request is not a negative judgment of the external reality, but a call not to be lost or to stray, not to perish from themselves, not to become an exile from their own bosom. Augustine refers to the problem of alienation as an outcome of not knowing oneself.

Return to yourself. Augustine calls for a return to the heart, because in the interiority of the heart there is the possibility to make decisions, to evaluate, to suffer, to enjoy, to feel, and to hope. For Augustine, the heart is the center of the person, the seat of emotions, thoughts, projects, the true home of man, where one feels at home. The withdrawal into the inner self is not an ascent into an impersonal unity, but a journey to a person, Jesus Christ, who heals our wounded hearts with the salve of his commandments of love. "In the inner man dwells Christ, in the inner man are you renewed after the image of God, in His own image recognize its Author."[39]

Transcend yourself. The return to our hearts is not the endpoint, but only a passage, through which we lift up our hearts to God. "Go back to your heart and from there to God."[40] Augustine emphasizes that returning to the inner self entails also transcending the inner self. In his *Confessions*, Augustine described his own pilgrimage to the inner life, realizing that before he was escaping from himself: "You were within me and I was outside, and there I sought for you and in my ugliness I plunged into the beauties that you have made. You were with me, and I was not with you."[41] By transcending himself and traveling to the ultimate level of his heart, Augustine discovered the place where God lives: "You were more inward to me than my most inward part; and higher than my highest."[42]

God Is Communion of Love

Augustine's spirituality of interiority is a spirituality of love grounded in the communion of the Holy Trinity. God is Love, "Communion of Love." Therefore, God wants to be with us. Through his conversion, Augustine discovered that God was more inside him than his innermost self, and higher than he was at his highest. God wants to be near us, without imposing himself, inviting us respectfully.

Love is the key that permits us to enter into the most intimate life of God. Augustine reminds us that the love of neighbor is the place where we meet God. God comes to us when we go to our neighbor. "Therefore love your neighbor; look at the source of your love of your neighbor; there you will see, as you may, God."[43] Augustine invites us to believe that through ecumenical dialogue and encounters, God comes to meet us. In fact, it is not we who approach God, but God who approaches us, inviting us to live in his communion of love. Through humility, we can prepare ourselves for that encounter. "The triune God, Father, and Son, and Holy Spirit, come to us while we are coming to Them…. They come to fill, we to contain: that our vision of Them may not be external, but inward; and Their abiding in us may not be transitory, but eternal."[44]

God reveals himself as the mystery of Trinity of communion among the divine persons. Being distinct, they are always in union, in intimate communion with each other. Christian life abides in God who is Communion of Love, Mystery of unity in diversity. For Augustine the most profound reality of God is that communion in which we may stay and live. God is Communion and this Communion is

the perfect realization of love. "For so great is the charity of
the Holy Spirit there, so great the peace of unity....If charity made one soul of so many souls, and one heart of so
many hearts, how great must be the charity between the
Father and the Son!"[45]

Augustine's spirituality of interiority reminds us that
we can enter into the mystery of the Holy Trinity, to abide
in the immutable and incomprehensible love of God. God
loved us before our own existence. Therefore, man owes
everything to God: the fact that I am a living being, that I
know, that I love, these are all gifts. We can only come to the
full development of our existence by loving God in return.
By the grace of God, we are able to love.

"With One Heart and One Soul Intent upon God"[46]

Augustine's spirituality of interiority has also an ecclesi-
sial dimension. One cannot confuse Augustine's spirituality
of interiority with intimacy, narcissism, egoism, or withdrawal into oneself. Augustine's concept of interiority is not
a private matter. In his *Confessions*, Augustine testified that
the closer he drew to the God of his heart, the closer he
drew to his neighbors, the better became his relations with
his family and friends and even with his enemies. His first
spontaneous reaction was to flee into solitude as soon as
peace came over him when he discovered the God of his
heart.[47] Through his conversion Augustine discovered true
community, the whole Christ, the Head and the Body, the
Church, the community in Acts 4:32, "of one heart and soul."
In his own monastery, Augustine tried to live the experience
of a community life through love. As Augustine experienced
the pain of a divided heart, he also felt the pain of the
divided Christian community in North Africa.

In his sermons Augustine refers many times to the first community of Jerusalem, which lived with one heart and one soul (Acts 4:32). The basic ideas of Augustine's *Rule* are inspired by the first community of Jerusalem as described in the Book of Acts 4:31–35. A good community is nothing else than the practice of love. In his concise style, Augustine always focuses on the root of things and the heart of man. The *Rule* follows the road of interiorization: the road to the heart.

The monastic tradition, and more specifically the insights and the *Rule* of Saint Augustine on community life, can be inspirational for Christian spirituality. The first Church of Jerusalem served as a model for Augustine's concept of religious community life. They were *of one heart and one mind*. The unity is not only the unity within their own hearts, but also a unity with others. The community should form a strong bond of love, expressing divine love. Division and dispersion are a negation of love. This mutual love leads to the all-embracing love of God. Augustine added "intent upon God," *in Deum* to the description from the Book of Acts: "of one heart and one soul" (Acts 4:32). The whole rule of Augustine is centered on the ideal of living harmoniously in one house, intent upon God, with one heart and one soul.

The realistic way, in which Augustine described community life in his sermons and in his *Rule*, can inspire us on the road toward a Christian way of life. It is not sufficient to eat at the same table and to live under the same roof. Community also requires openness to one another's inner life, one another's ideas, desires, hopes, and beliefs. Augustine underscored that love begins with giving and sharing what we possess. Growing together in love calls for relativizing personal property. It is remarkable how much attention Augustine spent on personal differences between members of the group, and with how much respect the individual personality of each was approached. Christian spirituality is based on loving respect of the uniqueness of everyone with each person's different gifts and needs, unique temperament, and irreplaceable character.

In his homilies, Augustine repeats that there is no community, no unity, no love, without humility. He feels that humility is a basic virtue. "I wish you to prepare for yourself no other way of seizing and holding the truth than that which has been prepared by Him who, as God, saw the weakness of our goings. In that way the first part is humility; the second, humility; the third, humility...so if you were to ask me...what are the instructions of the Christian religion, I would be disposed to answer always and only, Humility."[48] Pride is the great opponent of humility. Pride and love cannot tolerate each other.

A Spirituality of Concord or Harmony

Augustine's spirituality of interiority is also a spirituality of concord and harmony. Augustine understood unity as harmony. The unity of the Church takes the form of social and spiritual harmony, expressed in everyday life through the practice of charity. Through charity, multiplicity is led into unity. The fruit of unity in love is concord, oneness of heart.

We have been called to concord, to peace among ourselves. Augustine was fascinated by seeking together for the truth. He was convinced that if God is love, God is also truth. By searching together for truth, we are joined together in love: "Truth is not mine, nor his, nor hers, but belongs to all of us whom you call to share it in communion with him."[49]

Augustine considered unity as concord, harmony, a balanced peaceful rest among parts that are different from one another. He believed that truth is revealed through honest dialogue. Augustine aspired to harmony through fraternal dialogue in the time of the controversies with the Donatists, addressing them with a fraternal greeting, calling them brothers. He even invited the faithful to pray for them.

In his writings and homilies, Augustine promoted unity, emphasizing the intimate link between unity and love, Christ and the Church, the Head and the Body. Augustine makes unity a synonym for love, and a crucial proof of the Holy Spirit. Its opposite, the separation of the Church, was a sign of the Holy Spirit's absence. For Augustine the love for the unity of the Church was a pastoral priority. The daily contact with the Donatists profoundly marked his theology and his pastoral activities, and enabled him to apply a principle that is very important in pastoral life today: the distinction between the sin and the sinner. Augustine called them brothers not only as a sign of courtesy and sincere love, but because they possess the same "common goods" of the Catholics, even if they are in schism. With sincere fraternal spirit, he spoke with them about the mutual recognition of baptism. Augustine emphasizes that there is more that unites us than divides us. By calling schismatics brothers and recognizing the unicity of baptism, Augustine constitutes a considerable contribution to an effective progress in fraternal dialogue among Christians today.

Augustine's spirituality of concord can also be illustrated by his approach toward enemies. It was clear to him that we can never understand the depth of Christian faith if we are unable to love and pray for our enemies. Augustine invited the faithful to love their enemies to the end, that they may be our brothers. If we have to walk as Christ walked, that means walking the way of righteousness, the way of charity. Referring to Stephen, who followed the example of the Lord and prayed for his persecutors, Augustine concluded that Stephen had adhered to the unity of the dove. For Augustine, love is the main pillar of faith and Church. We cannot understand the Church outside the love of God for us. Walking as Christ means to pray for our enemies and not against them. We can never attempt to turn God into an executioner.

Augustine's spirituality of harmony shows the deep relationship between action and contemplation. He emphasizes the relationship and interaction between contemplation and action. Using various biblical figures, he described the two modes of Christian life: Martha and Mary, Peter and John, Rachel and Leah. Augustine, himself a monastic type, would have preferred the primacy of the contemplative life. Nevertheless, he recognized the value in faith of the active life and harmony between action and contemplation. By temperament, Augustine was not attracted to the active life of a leader of the Church. He confessed that he often envied the quiet life of an abbot, rather than his audience room. He was convinced that *the heart of Christian spirituality is to be found in love.* Congar speaks about *Ecclesia binoculata,* a Church with two eyes, meaning that she looks in two directions.[50] The Church looks to God, who is her source and the foundation of her life. At the same time, the Church looks to the world, which is needy and to whom she is sent, the world where there is often injustice and lovelessness. This dual orientation can be found in the *ora et labora* of Saint Benedict and the saying of Brother Roger of Taizé, "*lutte et contemplation.*"

The risen Lord shows us his wounds and says: "Peace be with you." As the apostles touched the wounds of the risen Lord, we may approach the risen Lord, realizing that he is already approaching us. Christian spirituality focuses on the way in which we all will be touched by the risen Lord spiritually, growing in faith, receiving his Spirit of immense love to embrace humanity and to promote peace and harmony.

Augustine reminds us that we are not alone in our pilgrimage. Christ is with us. He is our Way and our Light. When we practice mutual love, true peace lives in our heart, true peace, but not perfect peace on earth; we do yet possess it, but we live in hope. Augustine repeated frequently in his sermons that we need hope on our pilgrimage to the heavenly fatherland. If the journey begins to weigh on us, hope will sustain all our fatigue. "Listen and rejoice in hope, that, since the present is not a life to be loved, but to be tolerated, you may have the power of patient endurance amid all its tribulation."[51]

Augustine invites the faithful to abide together with him in the love of God and to love on their pilgrimage to the heavenly homeland. Regularly he uses the expression "love with me, by believing run with me."[52] For Augustine, Christ loved us in such a way, that we might through his example have God in us, that we might love one another, that God may be all in all.

CHAPTER 6

Saint Augustine as a Spiritual Guide

"A change of heart and holiness of life, along with public and private prayer for the unity of Christians, should be regarded as the soul of the whole ecumenical movement, and merits the name 'spiritual ecumenism.'"[1] With these words the Second Vatican Council affirmed that the ecumenical movement is essentially a spiritual movement.

The Second Vatican Council had in mind a return to the sources: Scripture, liturgy, and the Church fathers. One of the fathers featured most prominently in the documents of the Second Vatican Council is Saint Augustine. He is the most quoted father at the Council. On August 28, 1986, Pope John Paul II wrote *Augustinum Hipponensem*, an Apostolic Letter to the bishops, priests, religious families, and faithful of the whole Catholic Church on the occasion of the sixteenth centenary of the conversion of Saint Augustine, Bishop and Doctor of the Church.[2] Pope Benedict XVI regularly underscored that the teachings of Saint Augustine are a path for a Christian way of life today.

Augustine was a lover of the unity of the Church, a man of prayer and dialogue, a minister of the Word, a faithful shepherd deeply touched by the humility of Christ, undertaking the pilgrimage of the heart. He preached with a strong passion for Christ and the Church. Today he speaks to us as a spiritual guide, about the journey toward harmony through prayer, humility, the guidance of the Holy Spirit, the Pilgrim Church, and love for the poor. His witness is useful today, not only because of his words, but also because of his profound spirituality and pastoral wisdom.

PRAYER

Augustine emphasized that preaching needs to be supported by and founded upon prayer. The preacher is a mediator between the Word of God and the faithful. On the one hand, the minister stands face-to-face with God; on the other he stands face-to-face with the faithful. Augustine's dialogical preaching style had the tone of a familial conversation. It can encourage us to walk further on the road as pilgrims, crossing the mountains of misunderstanding, searching together for the horizon of Christian unity through prayerful dialogue.

Dialogue is a very important concept, which has been developed in twentieth-century philosophy. Man does not only have an encounter or a dialogue; he is encounter, he is dialogue.[3] Language is essentially dialogue. By speaking and through dialogue people become more human; language brings new ideas into life. Through dialogue new thoughts are born. Ecclesial documents, such as *Unitatis Redintegratio* and *Ut Unum Sint*, emphasized the importance of dialogue. Dialogue is more than an exchange of ideas; it is also an *exchange of gifts*.[4]

According to Augustine, a preacher must listen to the Word of God before he speaks. Both the preacher and the faithful need a deep and inner relationship with Christ. The preacher and the faithful are fellow students in one school, with one Teacher. Augustine's dialogical preaching is based upon listening together to God's Word in silence. With Augustine, we affirm that preaching must be nourished and inspired by Holy Scripture. Holy Scripture is food for the soul and the source of spiritual life. Christians can organize together a prayerful reading of Sacred Scripture. Dialogue has not only horizontal but also vertical dimensions. Prayer is the soul of dialogue.

Christian spirituality may be inspired by Augustine's concept of praying, which is *togetherness in silence with God*. Brother Roger of Taizé used to say that his brothers were not spiritual masters. *They are not called to give advice, but above all to be people who pray and who listen*. At Taizé, it is important that young people find someone who will listen to them. They have the opportunity to participate in simple prayer and can easily enter into the periods of silence during prayer. In a world where there is continual noise, the times of silence alternating with singing during the prayer at Taizé teaches them how to become quiet and at the same time how to inhabit this silence. The singing can penetrate deep into the heart of young people so that silence becomes prayer. They discover silence as richness, as a kind of discipline that can teach them how to listen. The brothers of Taizé are often impressed at how young people are able to remain together in silence with God for a long time. This way of praying touches the hearts of thousands of young people who come to Taizé.[5]

To Augustine, prayer is a matter of desire and yearning. Desire is the heart of prayer. Our prayer is a participation in the prayer of Christ. The ecumenical movement was driven by a spiritual movement built upon the desire of Christ for unity and whose underlying strength is the Week of Prayer for Christian Unity held every January, started by Paul Wattson. Father Paul Couturier proposed the Catholic observance, and now all Christians are able to pray together in a common universal week of prayer. They can be called pioneers of spiritual ecumenism.[6]

Augustine's *spirituality of togetherness* in listening together to the Word of God can be a source of inspiration for many ecumenical research institutes, where students of many denominations live, pray, and study together. There is no need to convince or try to convert the other. Through contact with one another, they deepen self-knowledge. Through mutual exchange, they grow in understanding and harmony. The enriching experience of ecumenical centers where we can study, pray, and live together reminds us that there is an *ecumenism of everyday life*. This is the shared commitment to the poor, the love of neighbor, the warmth of the hospitality and compassion, all fruits of the Holy Spirit. Many ecumenical institutes create places of encounter for young people, to open their hearts for new encounters. They offer a united and welcoming place that seeks to model an integrated approach to life, in which human community, study, and prayer, and care for the surrounding environment, all have their place. Young people share life and friendship, study and pray together. In these institutes, prayer is a source of spiritual nourishment. Common faith is expressed in prayers that lift the spirits of these young people as one voice, while they face their differences honestly and with respect.

The motif of the pilgrim's labyrinth of Chartres is that of a wheel. Prayer is an all-encompassing wheel that turns our lives to God. The spokes of the wheel refer to the different spiritual traditions of praying in different ecclesial communities. All these spokes are connected to the center, the axis of the wheel, Jesus Christ. The closer they come to Christ, the closer they come to each other. Through lived ecumenism, in common study and walking in dialogue and prayer, these students are as fellows of the same school.

They all have one Teacher, "the inner Master." This life together is based upon togetherness in and through prayer, in the hope of reaching a deeper relationship with God. The road to unity and harmony is through prayer.

HUMILITY

The second spiritual theme of Augustine as spiritual guide is the humility of Christ. Augustine never separated the Church from Christ. Christ is central in the preaching of Saint Augustine and his spirituality is a Christ-centered spirituality.

The ecumenical movement could draw sustaining inspiration by making a new start from Christ as Wounded Healer. Henri Nouwen develops the theme in his book *The Wounded Healer*. Christ made his own broken body the way to healing and new life. In our own woundedness, we become a source of healing and life for others. The Church must be a place wherein the wounded are healed just like the travelers' inn in the Samaritan parable.[7] Augustine's spirituality of togetherness is expressed in the fact that *hospitality becomes community*, that it creates a harmony based on the shared confession of our basic brokenness and on shared hope. Healing belongs to the heart of the Church. The Church is called to be a healing community, to share the wounds of its members and to be united with the oppressed, the marginalized, the corrupted, and the physically and mentally sick. Healing is the beginning of a new life in Christ, the restoration of the brokenness of life. It is building relationship and community. Through hospitality, a Christian community is a healing community. The host offers a friendly space where guests feel at home, where they share the pains and wounds of the past. Hospitality is a way in which the wounds become a source of healing.[8]

The theme of Christ as the Wounded Healer also deals with solidarity in suffering. Faced with the horror of concentration camps, theologian Jürgen Moltmann believed that God was a companion in suffering in the hell of Auschwitz. Solidarity in suffering has an important place in the concept of "minority" in Franciscan spirituality. This spirituality of minority invites us to embrace and to be advocates for God's most chosen—the poor, the oppressed, and the sick—and to create places of peace and reconciliation. When Augustine spoke about the healing activity of Christ, he was not only referring to the earthly Jesus but to the whole Christ. The cry of Christ dying on the cross becomes the cry of Christ for the unity of his Body, which is the Church. Augustine, who felt the pain of a divided Church, called the faithful to imitate the humble Christ. Christians feel the pain and the wounds of broken unity.

The humility of Christ is essential to Augustine's spirituality. Christ is the Master of humility. Christ is the humble Physician who came to heal the wounds of mankind with the medicine of humility, of self-emptying love. As the Divine Mediator, Christ reconciles all that divides humanity through humility. According to Congar, "The threshold of ecumenism can only be crossed on one's knees."[9] In 1963, at the end of the second session of the Second Vatican Council, Paul VI descended the steps of the papal throne in St. Peter's Basilica and laid the tiara on the altar in a dramatic gesture of humility and as a sign of the renunciation of human glory and power in keeping with the renewed spirit of the Council. Since then, none of his successors has worn a tiara. Pope Francis celebrated the Holy Thursday Mass of the Lord's Supper in *Casal del Marmo*, the juvenile detention facility in Rome and washed the feet of some of the young inmates.

In his homily, the Holy Father referred to Christ's caress, because Jesus came just for this, to serve us, to help us. Jean Vanier has reflected many times on the importance of the washing of feet in the community of L'Arche. He emphasizes that this gesture not only plays a role in their communities as sign of service, remission, and unity, but also in the encounters with Christians from different ecclesial communities. Augustine invites the faithful to imitate Christ, the Teacher of humility.[10] Christ's humility is an example for all Christians. The road to harmony is through humility.

THE HOLY SPIRIT

For Augustine, the Holy Spirit is the soul and the life of the Church. Augustine touches upon the charismatic dimension of the Church when he refers to the plurality of gifts. Following from Augustine, the Second Vatican Council brought about a rediscovery of the charisms. The Council emphasized that the Church has not only an institutional but also a charismatic dimension.[11] It can be said that the ecumenical movement is a charismatic event and an "undertaking of the Holy Spirit." The Holy Spirit is the motor of ecumenism. Where ecumenical consensus has been possible, it has always been experienced as a spiritual gift. The Holy Spirit is an agent of unity and reconciliation. The impressive 1964 meeting of Pope Paul VI and Patriarch Athenagoras I of Constantinople in Jerusalem was a significant step toward restoring communion between Rome and Constantinople. The mutual excommunications of 1054 were formally abolished one year later.

With the opening of the Second Vatican Council, Pope John XXIII expressed the hope of a new Pentecost, a new departure for the Church, with the view to future unity for the universal Church. Ecumenism is a vigil of Pentecost, the beginning of the transformation of a broken Christianity into a truly united Christianity according to nothing but the unity that Christ desires.

The Second Vatican Council returned to the original meaning of the role of the Holy Spirit in the Church, as Augustine often expressed, "The Holy Spirit works in the Church in the same way as the soul in the body; the soul plays the same role for the body as the Holy Spirit for the Body of Christ, the Church."[12] Therefore Christian spirituality is a matter of community spirituality, a spirituality of the Church as communion, of the Church as the people of God, the Body of Christ, the Temple of the Spirit. The Church does not possess the Spirit but the Spirit sustains and animates the Church.[13]

As a pastor and teacher, Augustine developed a spirituality in which the Spirit was the principle of life and harmony. The Holy Spirit leads to the renewal of creation. In the outpouring of the Spirit, new life is promised and given. In the theology of the indwelling of the Spirit, each creature is the dwelling place of the Spirit of God. Forests, rivers, insects, and birds exist and have value before God. They manifest the presence of the Spirit as the fruit of divine love.

The Holy Spirit also leads to the renewal of the Church under the guidance of the Holy Spirit, under the guidance of love. The heart of the Church is love. Because the Spirit is the bond of love that unites the Father and the Son for all eternity, he also unites the faithful in communion with each other. The road to harmony is under the guidance of the Holy Spirit.

THE PILGRIM CHURCH

Augustine developed a spirituality of togetherness of the Church in pilgrimage to the heavenly Jerusalem. Pilgrimage can be seen in relation to *synodality*: the people of God *on the way together*. *Synod* comes from the Greek *synhodos* and means "a common way." This refers to the whole Church that is called to follow the way of Jesus and to walk together in Christ.

Augustine developed a dynamic view on the Church as sacramental, spiritual, and eschatological communion. The idea of the Church as communion, as people of God, as taught by the Second Vatican Council, comes from the fathers of the Church, especially Saint Augustine.

The Church is a sacramental communion. Ecumenical spirituality is a sacramental spirituality. It is based on our common baptism by which we are already through the one Spirit members of the one Body of Christ and live in a profound spiritual communion as unity in faith. Augustine recognizes the validity of baptism administered outside the ecclesial community. This is a basic idea for the ecumenical movement today. For us today, common baptism is the common ground for all Christians. Augustine states that the Eucharist is the sacrament of unity, the bread of concord, and the bond of love. These words are repeated in the texts of the Second Vatican Council. Today we speak about the eucharistic ecclesiology of communion. Baptism is oriented toward eucharistic sharing. In the one eucharistic bread, we become one ecclesial body. It is a painful reality that all who are engaged in the ecumenical movement cannot yet share at the Lord's Table. Even though we cannot yet celebrate the

Eucharist together, there is much that we can do. The Eucharist is the celebration of the mystery of faith. We can already share in spiritual communion when we attend a eucharistic celebration in a Church not yet in full communion with the Catholic Church. Important steps can be taken to make full use of ecumenical forms of the Liturgy of the Word, Vespers, prayers for peace, memorial services inspired by Taizé, services that recall the worshippers' baptism, and ecumenical pilgrimages.[14]

Augustine described the Church as a spiritual communion, referring to the unifying activity of the Holy Spirit, who keeps the Church together. Augustine developed a community-spirituality as that of unity within diversity, a unity in concordance with the model of the Trinity, one God in three persons, existing in an intimate exchange of love. The Second Vatican Council took up this thought further and described the concept of *communio* as the most profound mystery of the Church, modeled as an icon of the Trinity. Different steps toward a spiritual communion of unity in diversity have been undertaken. Brother Roger of Taizé created the "pilgrimage of trust" as a global pilgrimage of reconciliation. In the community of L'Arche, the disabled are a unifying factor. Through their presence, the disabled help us to realize that all human beings have their own fragility and wounds. In this sense, they create a togetherness of common humanity.

According to Augustine, the Church is also an eschatological communion. Drawing from Saint Augustine, the Second Vatican Council rediscovered the eschatological dimension of the Church and developed a dynamic view of the Church as a Pilgrim Church, people of God on the move, undertaking a pilgrimage between *already* and *not yet*. The Trinity is the origin and the homeland of the Pilgrim Church.

Lumen Gentium evokes Augustine's thoughts on the Church, which embraces in its bosom sinners and saints, which needs to be purified, and which is called to follow the way of penance and renewal.[15] No harmony is possible without a change of heart and sanctification of personal life. Without conversion, penance, and renewal, there can be no dialogue and unity. Only through a real pilgrimage, which includes conversion, can the goal of unity be achieved. The Church is always in need of being purified, which must constantly take the way of conversion.

Christian unity is a way of living the communion of saints. Building bridges is a spiritual process and calls for openness of heart and sanctification of life. To work for harmony means to work for the holiness of the Church. Through its pilgrimage in time and history, the Church becomes what she already is: one holy Church.

Emphasizing the importance of reconciliation, the Second Vatican Council asked forgiveness for the faults of the past: *Unitatits Redintegratio* expressed the necessity of examining one's own faithfulness to Christ's will for the Church and of undertaking the task of renewal and reform. In *Tertio Millennio Adveniente*, John Paul II expressed the hope that the Jubilee Year of 2000 would be the occasion of purifying the memory of the Church from all forms of counter-witness and scandals.[16] John Paul II underlined that if we acknowledge the weaknesses of the past, this can help us to strengthen our faith and can alert us to face today's temptations and challenge us to meet them.

It is not possible to remove all tensions of the past immediately. Therefore, we have to work gradually, by healing the wounds, by lifting excommunications, by building bridges of peace. During the pilgrimage on earth, the churches have to come closer to each other in their lives: pray together, work together, live together. The churches are called to live focused on forgiveness, peace, and reconciliation. Conversion implies a change of heart and mind, which is necessary for the purification of our memories.

Singing also creates togetherness, a *concordia*, a harmony as can be seen in national anthems, at sporting events such as the Olympics. Songs can join people together. Music possesses a unifying power. Augustine describes a chorus as the union of singers. A chorus has to sing in concord. "The whole world is now the chorus of Christ."[17] In the Syriac liturgy, the communal aspect is strongly expressed through singing together. Praying and singing bring people closer to each other.

CHARITY

The fifth spiritual theme of Augustine as spiritual guide is Trinitarian love. For Augustine, the unity of the Church is grounded in the Trinitarian love among Father, Son, and Holy Spirit.

One may ask which perspectives of Augustine's vision of the Church, based in the Trinitarian love and rediscovered in the Second Vatican Council, can help the search for Christian unity. First, the Trinitarian origin of ecclesial communion reminds us that Christian unity is a gift from God. Second, the Trinitarian form of ecclesial communion shows us that Christian unity should not be conceived as uniformity but as a unity in diversity. Third, the Pilgrim Church needs to develop a constant openness to the words of Jesus "that all may be one," that their promise may become reality.

Christian spirituality can also be understood as a spirituality of togetherness through ecclesial charity for the poor, for those suffering from lack of housing and the unequal distribution of wealth. On our pilgrimage toward Christian unity, we engage our brothers and sisters of the other churches and ecclesial communities. Ecumenical visits provide an occasion not only for theological exchange, but also create a culture of friendship in a spirit of brotherhood and evangelical fraternity. Ecumenical encounters offer the possibility of welcoming others and being received by others. Mutual hospitality allows for a continual enrichment and fruitful encounter, and helps to resolve common problems concerning human life and society, and practical difficulties facing the Church. The pilgrimage to Christian unity is not indifferent to the concrete realities of the various Christian communities. For example, it is concerned with the common use of worship spaces and with questions of social justice, poverty, racism, and violence. Ecclesial charity aims to develop a culture of hospitality and friendship, encouraging the sharing of both joy and sadness among Christians. In this sense, we are always called to lighten one another's burdens.

Augustine's spirituality of ministry can be a guide for a Christian way of life and offers some basic attitudes for all those who exercise a ministry in the Church. The first anchor is Augustine's constant reference to Christ, the Good Shepherd, when he speaks about ministry. In exercising ministry, Christ must be at the center. The ministry of service through humility and love is a second anchor. The third anchor is the ministry of unity, which is a fruit of charity.

Augustine's spirituality of ministry, which is a ministry of love, can inspire us to understand the Petrine ministry spiritually as a primacy of love. The discussion on the Petrine ministry is one of the most difficult in ecumenical dialogue. Paul VI and John Paul II spoke openly about the paradoxical reality that the primacy of Peter, which is in the service of unity, can be considered as the greatest obstacle to broader Christian unity. During the last few years, in the context of globalization and in the growing awareness that all the churches now face the same challenges such as secularism, economic crisis, and threat to peace, the idea is growing on the ecumenical level that there should be a ministry of unity in the Church.

In his ecumenical encyclical *Ut Unum Sint*, John Paul II extended a revolutionary invitation to fraternal dialogue on the future exercise of primacy: "I insistently pray the Holy Spirit to shine his light upon us, enlightening all the Pastors and theologians of our Churches, that we may seek—together, of course—the forms in which this ministry may accomplish a service of love recognized by all concerned."[18] Pope John Paul II invited Church leaders and theologians to engage with him in a patient and fraternal dialogue on this subject. Augustine also can inspire us here.

Augustine's spirituality is also a spirituality of concord and harmony. The unity of the Church takes the form of social and spiritual harmony, expressed in everyday life through the practice of charity. Through charity, multiplicity is led into unity. The fruit of unity in love is concord, oneness of heart. Unity becomes a synonym for love and a crucial proof of the Holy Spirit. For Augustine, the love for the unity of the Church was a pastoral priority. His spirituality of togetherness, his call to integrity and the purification of the heart, the way to interiority leads to an authentic testimony of charity. The road to unity is through charity.

It is recommended when starting a pilgrimage that one should not begin with a quick walk, because patience is required in order to find the right rhythm. Likewise it can be said that those traveling along the road to Christian unity need time to learn to walk together, day by day, as pilgrims who realize that they walk without yet seeing the final destination, the vision of full unity. Many pilgrims begin their journey by undertaking the labyrinth of Chartres, which can be considered a symbol of Christian unity. This labyrinth is composed of different twists and curves, which represent our search for God. Christian unity also has many difficulties, challenges, or curves. When we arrive at each curve on the labyrinth and follow our road, we can have the impression that we have taken a step backward, but in fact, we have actually made progress. An apparent decline is a step forward. We should simply take further steps, with patience, confidence, and love. Additionally there is no orientation problem. We are never far from the center, because every step we take represents a further step in the right direction. We just have to follow our road, with patience and confidence. We have to go on, to continue, to make progress; we cannot hesitate. We are always on the way. Our journey has a goal *that all may be one*, but the road is long and winding. Progress can be difficult to see. Growth in faith and trust is not measurable. What matters is the confidence that we are moving, that the Lord Jesus himself leads us as a guide in the night. The heart of the pilgrim's labyrinth is a blossoming flower, whereas in ancient labyrinths there was a monster in the center, something scary or menacing. The pilgrim's labyrinth puts Christ at the center of all the turns of life. In Christ there is no fear. Whoever lives in the love of Christ, is freed from all fear. Love really unites us with God and strengthens the bonds among us, until this unity reaches completion in heaven.

Notes

INTRODUCTION

1. *Tractate*, 35, 9. Excerpts from the *Tractates* of Saint Augustine on the Gospel of John are from New Advent, Fathers of the Church, http://www.newadvent.org/fathers/1701.htm.

2. Cf. Gabriel Marcel, *Homo Viator: Introduction to a Metaphysic of Hope* (South Bend, IN: St. Augustine's Press, 2010).

3. Augustine, *Confessions*, 10, 8, 15.

4. Benedict XVI, *Visit to the Cathedral of Santiago de Compostela: Address of the Holy Father Benedict XVI*, Apostolic Journey to Santiago de Compostela and Barcelona, November 6, 2010. http://www.vatican.va/holy_father/benedict_xvi/speeches /2010/november/documents/hf_ben-xvi_spe_20101106_cattedrale -compostela_en.html.

CHAPTER I

1. Cf. Agostino Trapè, *Saint Augustine: Man, Pastor, Mystic* (New York: Catholic Book Publishing, 1986), 149.

2. Augustine, *Sermon*, 120, 2–3.

3. Ibid., 311, 4.

4. Cf. Marie François Berrouard, *Introduction aux homélies de Saint Augustin sur l'Évangile de Saint Jean* (Paris: Institut d'É- tudes Augustiniennes, 2004), 27–38, 103–14.

5. *Tractate*, 6, 4.

6. Cf. Tarsicius J. Van Bavel, *Bij het zestiende eeuwfeest van Augustinus' bekering: "Veel te laat heb ik jou lief gekregen": Leven en*

werk van Augustinus van Hippo (Heverlee-Leuven: Augustijns Historisch Instituut, 1986), 52–59.

    7. *Tractate*, 20, 1.

    8. Cf. Ibid., 15, 1.

    9. Ibid., 18, 6.

    10. Cf. Ibid., 2, 1.

    11. Ibid., 1, 7.

    12. Cf. Ibid., 4, 15.

    13. Ibid., 4, 16.

    14. *Sermon*, 261, 2.

    15. *Tractate*, 16, 3.

    16. Cf. Ibid., 2, 1.

    17. Cf. Martin Schrama, *Augustinus. De binnenkant van zijn denken* (Zoetermeer: Meinema, 1999), 51.

    18. *Confessions*, 9, 2, 3.

    19. Cf. *Sermon*, 262, 2.

    20. Augustine, *De Doctrina Christiana*, 4, 15, 32.

    21. *Tractate*, 4, 16.

    22. Cf. Pope John Paul II, *Ut Unum Sint* (May 25, 1995), 28.

    23. *Tractate*, 40, 10.

    24. Ibid.

    25. Ibid., 59, 3.

    26. Ibid., 26, 2–5.

    27. Ibid., 110, 2.

    28. Ibid., 111, 1.

    29. Cf. *Sermon*, 105, 1.

    30. *Tractate*, 26, 4.

CHAPTER 2

    1. Cf. Rowan Williams, "Augustine on Christ and the Trinity" in *Saint Augustine*, ed. Tarsicius J. Van Bavel and Bernard Bruning (Brussels: Mercatorfonds, 2007), 239–42.

    2. *Tractate*, 2, 2.

    3. Ibid., 33, 4.

    4. Ibid., 13.

5. Ibid., 123, 5.

6. Ibid., 47, 3.

7. Ibid., 13, 4.

8. Ibid., 2, 3.

9. Ibid., 35, 9.

10. Cf. Rudolph Arbesmann, "Christ the *Medicus Humilis* in St. Augustine," *Traditio* 10 (1954): 1–28.

11. Cf. *Tractate*, 35, 6.

12. Ibid., 25, 16.

13. Cf. Ibid., 1, 12; 35, 3.

14. Cf. Ibid., 3, 13.

15. Cf. Ibid., 120, 2.

16. Ibid.

17. Cf. Ibid., 41, 13.

18. Cf. Ibid., 119, 4.

19. Ibid., 58, 4.

20. Cf. Deborah Wallace Ruddy, "The Humble God. Healer, Mediator, and Sacrifice," *Logos: A Journal of Catholic Thought and Culture* 7, no. 3 (2004): 87–108.

21. *Tractate*, 15, 6.

22. Ibid., 58, 5.

23. Ibid., 6, 10.

CHAPTER 3

1. Cf. Elizabeth A. Dreyer, *Holy Power, Holy Presence: Rediscovering Medieval Metaphors for the Holy Spirit* (New York/Mahwah, NJ: Paulist Press, 2007), 44.

2. Cf. *Tractate*, 52, 6.

3. Augustine, *De Trinitate*, 15, 19, 34.

4. Cf. Augustine, *Enarrationes in Psalmos*, 67, 16; 130, 6.

5. Cf. *Tractate*, 27, 6.

6. Cf. Dreyer, *Holy Power, Holy Presence*, 46–52.

7. Cf. Augustine, *De Civitate Dei*, XIV, 28.

8. Cf. Raniero Cantalamessa, *The Mystery of Pentecost* (Collegeville, MN: Liturgical Press, 2001), 8–18.

9. Cf. Pope Paul VI, *Unitatis Redintegratio* (November 21, 1964), 2.

10. Pope Paul VI, *Ad Gentes* (December 7, 1965), 4.

11. Cf. Dreyer, *Holy Power, Holy Presence*, 57–60.

12. Cf. *Tractate*, 74, 2.

13. Cf. Ibid., 27, 11.

14. Ibid., 6, 10.

15. Cf. Ibid., 6, 3; Cf. Rom 8:26.

16. *Tractate*, 6, 2.

17. Cf. Ibid., 33, 5.

18. Ibid., 121, 5.

19. Cf. Ibid., 94, 5.

20. Cf. Ibid., 94, 2.

21. Ibid., 106, 6.

22. Ibid., 94, 2.

23. Ibid., 93, 1.

24. Ibid., 96, 4.

25. Ibid., 85, 3.

26. Cf. Ibid., 96, 4.

27. Ibid., 96, 5.

CHAPTER 4

1. Cf. *Tractate*, 108, 5.

2. Cf. Ibid., 47, 5.

3. Cf. Ibid., 6, 10.

4. Katholieke Studenten Actie, KSA Noordzeegouw.

5. *Tractate*, 21, 8.

6. Cf. Marcel Neusch, *Saint Augustin: L'amour sans mesure* (Saint-Maur: Parole et Silence, 2001), 83–84.

7. *Tractate*, 15, 3.

8. William Harmless, SJ, "Baptism," in *Augustine through the Ages: An Encyclopedia*, ed. Allan Fitzgerald, et al. (Grand Rapids, MI: W. B. Eerdmans, 2009), 88. Cf. *Tractate*, 6, 15.

9. *Tractate*, 26, 13.

10. Cf. Ibid., 26, 17.

11. Cf. Pope Paul VI, *Lumen Gentium* (November 21, 1964), 4. Cf. *Unitatis Redintegratio*, 2.

12. Cf. Tarsicius J. Van Bavel, "Church," in *Augustine through the Ages*, 169–76.

13. Cf. *Tractate*, 35, 9.

14. Cf. Ibid., 40, 10.

15. Ibid., 30, 7.

16. Ibid., 6, 2.

17. Cf. Neusch, *Saint Augustin*, 129–30.

18. *Sermon*, 63, 2.

19. Ibid., 63, 3.

20. *Tractate* 35, 9: "By believing run with me."

21. Cf. Trapè, *Saint Augustine*, 253.

22. Cf. *Tractate*, 53, 12.

23. Cf. Benedict XVI, *Eucharistic Concelebration: Homily of His Holiness Benedict XVI*, Pastoral Visit to Vigevano and Pavia, 'Orti Borromaici' Esplanade Pavia, Third Sunday of Easter, April 22, 2007, http://www.vatican.va/holy_father/benedict_xvi/homilies/2007/documents/hf_ben-xvi_hom_20070422_pavia_en.html.

24. Cf. *Confessions*, 3, 4, 7.

25. Ibid., 8, 12, 29.

26. Ibid.

27. *Sermon*, 340, 3.

28. Benedict XVI, *Homily, Pastoral Visit to Vigevano*.

29. Benedict XVI, *General Audience*, Paul VI Audience Hall, Ash Wednesday, February 21, 2007, http://www.vatican.va/holy_father/benedict_xvi/audiences/2007/documents/hf_ben-xvi_aud_20070221_en.html.

30. *Lumen Gentium*, 8.

31. Cf. *Tractate*, 22, 3.

32. Ibid., 65, 1.

33. Ibid.

34. *Sermon*, 336, 1.

35. *Enarratio In Psalmum*, 86, 1.

36. *Enarratio In Psalmum*, 66, 6.

37. *Sermon*, 34.

CHAPTER 5

1. Cf. Berrouard, *Introduction aux homélies de Saint Augustin*, 209–10. Cf. *Tractate*, 32, 9.
2. Cf. *Tractate*, 21, 8.
3. Cf. Ibid., 65, 2.
4. Cf. Ibid., 12, 9.
5. Ibid., 35, 9.
6. Cf. Raymond F. Canning, *The Unity of Love for God and Neighbour in St. Augustine* (Heverlee-Leuven: Augustinian Historical Institute, 1993), 251.
7. Cf. Tarsicius J. Van Bavel, "Love," in *Augustine through the Ages*, 512–13.
8. Cf. *Tractate*, 17, 8.
9. *Sermon*, 66, 5.
10. Ibid., 340, 1.
11. Ibid., 355, 4, 5.
12. *Tractate*, 41, 13.
13. Cf. Schrama, *Augustinus*, 152–63.
14. Cf. Joseph T. Lienhard, "Friendship," in *Augustine through the Ages*, 372.
15. Cf. Carole Straw, "Martyrdom," in *Augustine through the Ages*, 538–42.
16. Cf. Dreyer, *Holy Power, Holy Presence*, 52–53. Cf. *Tractate*, 92, 9.
17. *Confessions*, 13, 7, 8.
18. *Tractate*, 77, 5.
19. Cf. Ibid., 103, 3.
20. Ibid., 77, 3.
21. Cf. Joseph T. Lienhard, "Ministry," in *Augustine through the Ages*, 567–69.
22. *Tractate*, 40, 10.
23. Augustine, *Epistula*, 217.
24. *Sermon*, 340, 1. The current Bishop of Bruges, Bishop Jozef De Kesel, took this quote as his motto: *Vobiscum Christianus*.
25. Cf. Schrama, *Augustinus*, 295–306.
26. *Tractate*, 5, 15.

27. Ibid., 9, 10.
28. Cf. *Sermon*, 216, 9
29. Cf. Van Bavel, "Church," in *Augustine through the Ages*, 174.
30. Cf. *Tractate*, 118, 4.
31. Cf. Ibid., 13, 13.
32. *Sermon*, 269, 3–4.
33. *Tractate*, 123, 5
34. Ibid.
35. Cf. Trapè, *Saint Augustine*, 148. Cf. *Tractate*, 123, 5.
36. *Tractate*, 18, 10.
37. Ibid.
38. Ibid.
39. Ibid.
40. *Sermon*, 311, 13.
41. *Confessions*, 10, 27.
42. Ibid., 3, 6, 11.
43. *Tractate*, 17, 8.
44. Ibid., 76, 4.
45. Ibid., 14, 9.
46. Augustine, *Praeceptum*, 1.
47. Cf. Thomas F. Martin, "Augustinian Spirituality," in *Saint Augustine*, 255–56.
48. *Epistula*, 118, 3, 22.
49. *Confessions*, 12, 25, 34.
50. Cf. Yves Congar, *Le Concile au jour le jour: Quatrième session* (Paris: Cerf, 1966), 27.
51. *Tractate*, 111, 1.
52. Ibid., 35, 9.

CHAPTER 6

1. *Unitatis Redintegratio*, 8.
2. Cf. John Paul II, *Augustinum Hipponensem*, Apostolic Letter, 1986, http://www.vatican.va/holy_father/john_paul_ii/apost_letters/documents/hf_jp-ii_apl_26081986_augustinum-hipponensem_en.html.

3. Cf. Walter Kasper, *That They May All Be One: The Call to Unity Today* (London: Burns & Oates, 2004), 35.

4. Cf. *Ut Unum Sint*, 28.

5. Cf. Olivier Clément, *Taizé: A Meaning to Life* (Chicago: GIA Publications, 1997), 53.

6. Cf. James F. Puglisi, "Prayer for Christian Unity in the Twentieth Century," in *A Century of Prayer for Christian Unity*, ed. Catherine E. Clifford (Grand Rapids, MI: Eerdmans, 2009), 49–50.

7. Cf. *Tractate*, 41, 13.

8. Cf. Henri Nouwen, *The Wounded Healer: Ministry in Contemporary Society* (Garden City, NY: Doubleday, 1970), 82–83.

9. Yves Congar, *Dialogue between Christians* (London: Chapman, 1996), 130.

10. Cf. Jean Vanier, *The Scandal of Service: Jesus Washes Our Feet* (Toronto: Novalis, 1996).

11. Cf. *Lumen Gentium*, 4, 7, 12, 49.

12. *Sermon*, 267, 4. Cf. *Lumen Gentium*, 7.

13. Cf. Kasper, *That They May All Be One*, 100, 156.

14. Cf. Walter Kasper, *A Handbook of Spiritual Ecumenism* (Hyde Park, NY: New City Press, 2007).

15. Cf. *Lumen Gentium*, 8.

16. John Paul II, *Tertio Millennio Adveniente*, Apostolic letter, 2000, 33, http://www.vatican.va/holy_father/john_paul_ii/apost_letters/documents/hf_jp-ii_apl_10111994_tertio-millennio-adveniente_en.html.

17. *Enarratio in Psalmum*, 149, 4.

18. *Ut Unum Sint*, 95.

Bibliography

DOCUMENTS OF THE CHURCH

The Second Vatican Council

Second Vatican Council. *Lumen Gentium*, Dogmatic Constitution on the Church, 1964.
————. *Unitatis Redintegratio*, Decree on Ecumenism, 1964.

Papal Statements

Benedict XVI. *Church Fathers: From Clement of Rome to Augustine.* Grand Rapids, MI: Eerdmans, 2009.
John Paul II. *Ut Unum Sint*, Encyclical Letter, 1995.

Other

Pontifical Council for Promoting Christian Unity. *Directory for the Application of Principles and Norms on Ecumenism.* Vatican City: Vatican Press, 1993.
United States Catholic Conference of Catholic Bishops. *Catechism of the Catholic Church.* Washington, 2000, 2nd ed. Revised in accordance with the official Latin text (Vatican City: Libreria Editrice Vaticana, 1994).

TRANSLATIONS

Augustine (Saint). *Tractates on the Gospel of John* (5 vol.), translated by J. W. Rettig, The Fathers of the Church 78.79.88.90.92, Washington 1988–95.

STUDIES ON SAINT AUGUSTINE

Arbesmann, Rudolph. "Christ the *Medicus Humilis* in St. Augustine." *Traditio* 10 (1954): 1–28.

Berrouard, Marie-François. *Introduction aux homélies de Saint Augustin sur l'Évangile de Saint Jean.* Paris: Institut d'Études Augustiniennes, 2004.

Canning, Raymond F. *The Unity of Love for God and Neighbour in St. Augustine.* Heverlee/Leuven: Augustinian Historical Institute, 1993.

Congar, Yves. *I Believe in the Holy Spirit* (translated from French). New York: Seabury Press/London: G. Chapman, 1983.

Dreyer, Elizabeth A. *Holy Power, Holy Presence. Rediscovering Medieval Metaphora for the Holy Spirit.* New York/Mahwah, NJ: Paulist Press, 2007.

Fitzgerald, Allan D. and John C. Cavadini, eds. *Augustine through the Ages: An Encyclopedia.* Grand Rapids, MI: W. B. Eerdmans Publishing, 2009.

Hand, Thomas A. *Augustine on Prayer.* New York: Catholic Book Publishing, 1986.

Neusch, Marcel. *Initiation à Saint Augustin, maître spiritual.* Paris: Éditions du Cerf, 2003.

———. *Saint Augustin, L'amour sans mesure.* Langres: Parole et Silence, 2001.

Ruddy, Deborah W. "The Humble God: Healer, Mediator, and Sacrifice." *Logos: A Journal of Catholic Thought and Culture* 7/3 (2004): 87–108.

Schrama, Martijn. *Augustinus. De binnenkant van zijn denken.* Zoetermeer: Meinema, 1999.

Trapè, Agostino. *Saint Augustine: Man, Pastor, Mystic.* New York: Catholic Book Publishing, 1986.

Van Bavel, Tarsicius. J., and Bernard Bruning, eds. *Saint Augustine.* Brussels: Mercatorfonds/Heverlee: Augustinian Historical Institute, 2007.

———. *Veel te laat heb ik jou liefgekregen. Leven en werk van Augustinus.* Heverlee/Leuven: Augustijns Historisch Instituut, 1986.

STUDIES ON SPIRITUAL ECUMENISM AND CONTEMPORARY SPIRITUALITY

Cantalamessa, Raniero. *Come, Creator Spirit: Meditations on the Veni Creator.* Collegeville, MN: Liturgical Press, 2003.

———. *The Mystery of Pentecost Creator* (translated from Italian). Collegeville, MN: Liturgical Press, 2001.

Clément, Olivier. *Taizé: A Meaning to Life* (translated from French). Chicago, IL: GIA Publications, 1997.

Communauté de Taizé. *Choose to Love: Brother Roger of Taizé: 1915–2005.* Taizé: Ateliers et Presses de Taizé, 2007.

Edwards, Denis. *Breath of Life: A Theology of the Creator Spirit.* Maryknoll, NY: Orbis Books, 2004.

Healey, Charles J. *Christian Spirituality: An Introduction to the Heritage.* New York: Alba House, 1999.

Kasper, Walter. *A Handbook of Spiritual Ecumenism.* Hyde Park, NY: New City Press, 2007.

———. *That They May All Be One: The Call to Unity Today.* London/New York: Burns & Oates, 2004.

McGrath, Alister E. *Christian Spirituality: An Introduction.* Oxford: Blackwell, 1999.

Nouwen, Henri. *The Wounded Healer: Ministry in Contemporary Society.* Garden City, NY: Doubleday, 1970.

Puglisi, James F. "Prayer for Christian Unity in the Twentieth Century." In *A Century of Prayer for Christian Unity*, edited by

Catherine E. Clifford, 41–62. Grand Rapids, MI: Wm. B. Eerdmans, 2009.

Vanier, Jean. *Drawn into the Mystery of Jesus through the Gospel of John*. New York/Mahwah, NJ: Paulist Press, 2004.

————. *The Heart of L'Arche: A Spirituality for Every Day*. Toronto: Novalis, 2012.

————. *The Scandal of Service: Jesus Washes Our Feet*. Toronto: Novalis, 1996.